BOLTON WANDERERS

10 YEARS AT THE REEBOK

First published in Great Britain in 2007 by
The Breedon Books Publishing Company Limited
Breedon House, 3 The Parker Centre,
Derby, DE21 4SZ.

ISBN 978-1-85983-571-5

Printed and bound by Scotprint, Haddington.

BOLTON WANDERERS

10 YEARS AT THE REEBOK

BY TONY GARNER

Contents

Acknowledgements   **6**

Foreword   **7**

Introduction
Pre-bok   **8**

Chapter One
1997-98 **It Started With a Miss**   **14**

Chapter Two
1998–99 **The Watford Gap**   **36**

Chapter Three
1999–2000 **The Second Coming**   **56**

Chapter Four
2000–01 **Going Up, Definitely Maybe**   **78**

Chapter Five
2001–02 **Surprise Packages**   **102**

Chapter Six
2002–03 **Natural Born Footballer**   **124**

Chapter Seven
2003–04 **All You Need Is Love**   **147**

Chapter Eight
2004–05 **The Euro Visionaries**   **167**

Chapter Nine
2005–06 **We Have Lift Off**   **191**

Chapter 10
2006–07 **Taking Charge**   **212**

Roll of Honour   **238**

Acknowledgements

Thanks to Debra Mitchell from Apple Transcription and the team at Viva PR, who together helped me bring this book to life. Thanks also to Wanderers' Communications Manager Danny Reuben, who came up with the idea then entrusted me to develop it. Without Danny and his team, Paul Holliday and Keeley Temple, it would have been a real struggle. My special thanks must go to Paul Mulderrig for his advice and encouragement along the way. Of course, I am grateful to everyone who contributed – players, staff and supporters. And one final word of thanks to my smashing wife Sandra, who had to put up with an absent husband during the months of research and writing. I'm back now.

Most pictures have been supplied by Action Images.

Tony Garner, May 2007

Foreword

When I was asked to put a few words together to celebrate the 10th birthday of the Reebok stadium, my first reaction was surprise. It's hard to believe that the Reebok is 10 years old. It looks just as magnificent today as when it was first built.

And what an incredible 10 years it has been.

It has been a fantastic time to be a Bolton Wanderers supporter. We've seen some great games, signed some world-class players and enjoyed some wonderful moments.

In recent times, my boxing career has taken me all over the world, and no matter where I travel people have heard of Bolton thanks to the exploits of the men from the Reebok.

It's a great stadium and a fitting home for a great club. Well done to all involved for making the first 10 years so memorable. Here's to the next 10!

Amir Khan

Pre-bok

17 March 1973 marked the start of my lifelong obsession with Bolton Wanderers Football Club. We were playing Rochdale in a Division Three game. It was sunny, and I was standing there on the Embankment End with my dad, who chain-smoked his way through a packet of Senior Service and said 'Jesus' a lot. The latter upset me much more than the smoking. I was a good St Thomas of Canterbury lad at the time. I remember the score – Wanderers won 2–1. I remember the smells – stale tobacco, Thwaites' bitter and Bazooka Joe chewing gum. I remember the excitement of walking along Manchester Road among a crowd, stopping the traffic, because we, the fans, had a divine right of way. I remember the little caravan selling the Buff with smudgy ink reports from other games. I even remember that Charlie Wright was in goal. Not that he did anything spectacular that day. Just his name stuck with me. It seemed so perfect for a goalkeeper. It's

a name that's evocative of an era. On the internet you won't find much else about that match outside the bald facts of the result and date.

Don't ask me how I know all this. It's just lodged there in my brain. All the other important stuff I learned at school, like quadratic equations and conjugated French verbs, has long since been forgotten.

Of course, the events that day took place at Burnden Park. Over the years it became a shrine. Even passing Burnden on the bus from school used to give me a thrill. It had character. It had history. It had four huge floodlight pylons standing guard over it.

But 20 years on the club announced they were packing up and moving on to pastures new. Despite my affection for the old ground, I knew it made sense. For the same ground that had left a six-year-old awe-struck was by now a dilapidated museum piece. It was slowly falling down around us and forever blighted by an ugly supermarket right on the spot where I had made my terrace debut alongside my dad.

In the wake of the Taylor Report into the Hillsborough disaster in 1989, the architecture of English football was undergoing a revolution. New stands were springing up all over. Wanderers were being left behind. On the field, too, the game was changing. In 1992 the Premier League was launched, giving the traditional game a new gloss.

Cash-strapped and hamstrung by an antiquated stadium, what Wanderers desperately needed was a new vision, and the Bolton board, led by chairman Gordon Hargreaves, was acutely aware of it. Post-Taylor football grounds were supposed to be safer. Burnden Park, with its timber main stand and decaying structures around it, barely managed to get a safety certificate, despite the efforts of Frank Smith and director Graham Ball, whose first game as a supporter was the Burnden Disaster. Burnden Park was on its last legs, yet the club was struggling to find enough money just to keep the team running. Redeveloping Burnden Park simply wasn't an option from both a financial or practical perspective.

Old Glory: Wanderers' former home Burnden Park back in March 1996.

In the late 1980s Bolton MBC had hit on the idea of creating a sports and leisure complex, which would act as a catalyst to bring jobs and investment to the town. Half a dozen potential sites were identified and eventually Wanderers were invited to get involved in discussions. The two organisations recognised the mutual benefits a partnership could create and so joined forces. After several years of discussions and negotiations, they selected Middlebrook, a 200-acre site on the edge of the Horwich and Lostock border.

The council's overriding consideration was that the whole development would create jobs, and before agreeing to provide the land to the club for a new stadium they insisted that Wanderers had to first agree to stringent conditions. These included: a restriction on the capacity because of the traffic flows on the nearby roads; the stadium had to provide community benefits, like an exhibition centre; matchday rail links and bus arrangements had to be put in place by the club; and the professional teams overseeing the construction would have to be agreed in advance by the council.

Perhaps most significantly, they also stated that the stadium had to be an architectural statement that would attract interest to the area.

However, when the plan for a new ground near Horwich was made public, it was greeted with almost universal horror. Local residents felt that house prices would suffer, many Bolton fans didn't want to leave Burnden Park for sentimental reasons and neighbouring councils in Wigan and Chorley felt the project, with shops, bars and restaurants, would harm their town centres.

While the planning saga dragged on, Ball and then club secretary Des McBain travelled extensively to look at new stadiums for ideas and potential pitfalls. Their main recommendation was for the stadium to have the potential for other commercial activity built into the design.

Eventually the planning battle was won, but it was a long drawn out affair. In total, the planning process took 11 years. Once agreed, however, work on the stadium was incredibly swift. The entire build took a whirlwind 11 months.

International stadium architects Lobb Associates were responsible for the design, and Birse Group was appointed to look after the construction. Jan Kozlowski, now Wanderers' facilities director, had spent 17 years with international building company Alfred McAlpine. He had worked on the Centenary Stand at Anfield and headed the team that rebuilt the Stretford End at Old Trafford.

'McAlpine had originally built the Kirklees Stadium in Huddersfield (now the Galpharm Stadium) and was keen to build the stadium at Bolton,' says Jan. 'It didn't win the contract, but was awarded the contract to build the pitch and the surrounding road. While I was at a site meeting, I met the club chairman Gordon Hargreaves and, without me knowing, he interviewed me. He offered me a job as the club's on-site engineer. Bolton didn't have anybody at the time who was knowledgeable in football ground construction, so I became the club's project manager and my brief was simple. Effectively, they said "Here's £25 million, these are the drawings, now go and build it!"

'The timescales were tight and weren't helped because the stadium is a complete one-off, with the West Stand being a completely different design to the East Stand in terms of how it is supported.

'Seeing the structure go up was absolutely fantastic. It was a phenomenal job to be involved in. It was a very fancy design and, despite the time pressure, we had to make certain changes, like adding larger generators to the process. The biggest change was that we ended up completing the whole of the East Stand. The original plan had been to leave it as a shell, but because it looked as though the club would be promoted to the Premier League the board decided to press ahead and complete that too.

'In order to get the local authority to approve the stadium, I asked the contractor to finish three days earlier than his contracted timescale. That way we could actually test it by having an event. We held a trial game which only lasted about half an hour each way. Season ticket holders were allowed in free of charge, and about 12,000 turned up. That trial allayed the concerns of a lot of people, not only at the club but those who had been involved in the construction process and the stadium management people too, as well as the local authority, the police and the ambulance services.'

With the construction phase well under way, Paul Fletcher, a former Bolton player who had played a leading role in making Huddersfield's new stadium a success, was appointed to help make sure Wanderers could take advantage of the commercial potential of their new base.

'One of the key things I managed to do early on was to persuade the directors about the importance of marketing the stadium itself – even before it had opened,' says Fletcher.

'One of my jobs was to look for a naming sponsor, and Reebok was an obvious one because of its links with the town. People had seen the money that was available in the United States through naming rights, but one of the key principles is that it is important to get that name across in the media. For example, the new Southampton stadium has been dubbed St Mary's by the media, and not the Friends Provident St Mary's Stadium. It was vitally important to get the right name, and with Reebok I think we did. It is a good name. It's a Bolton name.'

The council's insistence that the stadium had to be a landmark building fit in perfectly with the visions of Hargreaves's board and the prevailing thoughts on sports stadium design.

Welcome to the Reebok: the main entrance to Bolton's Reebok stadium.

'The Reebok was constructed at a time when architects started wanting to create something more than just a simple shed to house people. They wanted to make an attractive design statement too,' says Fletcher. 'I think they did that with the Reebok. It is, without doubt, a beautiful building, and the architectural awards that later stacked up only backed that up.

'It was a visionary idea to build a new stadium, but if you look at what has happened at all the places where new stadiums have been built, it tends to come at a cost. Leicester went down once they decided to move away from Filbert Street, Huddersfield struggled after they had built the McAlpine, and Sunderland went down after they had built their new stadium.

'But looking long term, you are preparing for the future and you have to ask yourself "Would the club be where they are today if they were still at Burnden Park?" and I think the answer is obvious.

'Building the Reebok was a very forward-thinking move because it allowed the club to flourish. It certainly must have attracted one or two players over the years and maybe even a manager.'

The truth is that building the Reebok was the club's only option for long-term survival. The stadium and the Middlebrook project has been a wonderful regeneration success story for the town, with more than 5,000 jobs created.

But the most incredible story is the one that has taken place on the football field. For no one could have predicted 10 years ago what a wonderful adventure the football club was embarking on.

This is the story of that journey.

Chapter One

1997–98

It Started With a Miss

A turning point – every self-respecting football season has one. But how many of these defining moments arrive as early as the very first home game, for crying out loud? It's a little like seeing Brad Pitt bite the dust before the opening credits have rolled! But that's precisely what we're dealing with here. One of the most pivotal moments in the stadium's history arrived less than an hour into its life as the new home of the Wanderers.

Bolton, in the shape of burly Northern Irish defender Gerry Taggart, were denied a goal, and ultimately victory, on their debut in the £30 million plus stadium simply because a linesman did not notice that Taggart's header had sent the ball a clear six inches over

Silent tribute: the Reebok opens on 1 September 1997 with a minute's silence in honour of Diana, Princess of Wales.

Critical incident: Everton defender Terry Phelan manages to clear a header from Gerry Taggart (hidden), but not before the ball crosses the line.

the line. Nine months on, that miss against Everton came back to haunt the club in the cruellest way possible – relegation.

More than 10 years may have elapsed, but there are ghosts in the Reebok's corridors still tormented by the 'goal that never was'. Theirs is a tale of what might have been. It might have been a victory. It might have been three points. It might have been survival. Sorry to spoil the chapter ending so early, but this isn't Roy of the Rovers; this is Bolton. The Great Escape never happened.

Instead, a campaign that started with such high hopes ended with the kind of soul searching that relegation always inflicts. The financial realities of the investment in the Reebok quickly dawned, and the slow break-up of a team was not far behind.

When the fall-out eventually settled, there were empty seats in the Reebok – in the stadium, in the boardroom and eventually in the manager's office. You might think we're racing ahead of ourselves here; however, you can draw a clear timeline to the traumatic events two years into the Reebok's life from the moment, just 60 minutes in, when the referee waved play on, despite Wanderers' cries of 'goal!'

There's a school of thought that suggests Colin Todd's departure in September 1999 and his subsequent replacement by Sam Allardyce may never have come about if the linesman had been a tad more observant in the Reebok curtain-raiser.

It was a pure *Sliding Doors* moment, when the destinies of several individuals in the Reebok story were altered forever.

There's a classic football platitude which states that such blunders even themselves out over the course of a season. But do they? Well, as far as the likes of Taggart, Todd and others are concerned, they didn't – not this time. They believe that Wanderers should have won the game against Everton that night. The natural conclusion of their argument is that Wanderers' relegation nine months later could have been avoided.

In a bitterly ironic twist in the tale, the team that escaped the drop on the last day was Everton. The men from Goodison Park, the beneficiaries of that opening night oversight, finished one vital place higher in the final table – saved by goal difference only. Wanderers went down. Relegated by six inches.

Bolton were experts in relegation. The club had been demoted from the Premier League two seasons previously. However, going into the 1997–98 campaign there were not unreasonable grounds to think that things may turn out a little differently. The feeling wasn't solely based on the highly-contagious optimism that seems to afflict every fan from Carlisle to Cardiff each August. The omens were seriously good. Bolton's promotion to the Premier League had been achieved at an incredible canter. Colin Todd's side had earned glowing reviews not only for their title-winning exploits but for the neat and tidy style of football they played along the way. Hard to believe now, but even the media appeared to have a soft spot for the Wanderers. Supporting the optimists' arguments was the fact that Todd had been able to spend the summer months recruiting record signings and England legends to bolster the title-winning side.

'We had won the old First Division in style,' recalls Todd. 'We had the title secured with five games to go, and it was a tremendous season. Nathan Blake and John McGinlay scored lots of goals between them, and we played some really entertaining, attacking football.' The latter was Todd's trademark: 'Of course, I believed in keeping clean sheets, but I also believed in trying to play the game with a little bit of style and panache. We wanted to entertain people as well.'

It's hard to present entertainment in the form of bare statistics, but a club record of 100 League goals and 98 points gained that promotion season says a lot. It certainly wasn't a title won by grinding out 1–0 wins.

Of course, for some supporters, brought up in their forefathers' footsteps, the nagging doubts over being uprooted from Burnden remained, but at the same time many others were bullish about our prospects. If the Championship, promotion and new signings weren't enough to inspire optimism, then there was always the Reebok itself. This wasn't just a new ground. The Reebok was one of the most amazing new sports stadiums built in the UK for decades – and it was Bolton's! It was a bold design statement that demanded attention. It said 'Look at us, we are Bolton Wanderers and we are proud of it.' So, this time the Premier League would be different, surely.

Todd, who had been consulted on the design and layout of certain aspects of the new ground, like the dressing rooms, sums the mood up thus: 'For the Reebok stadium's completion to coincide with us winning the League and gaining promotion was great. Great for the team, for the fans, for the town and great from a financial perspective for the club.'

Maybe this optimism was infectious. Certainly, the Reebok's glittering edifice appeared to have a hypnotic hold over everyone concerned. In April 1997, with promotion to the Premier League confirmed, Wanderers had announced a reverse takeover by Mosaic Investments – and put their name on the London Stock Exchange, a fashionable move for football clubs in that era. The deal immediately made around £10 million available, which was used to provide the final slice of funding for the stadium and helped Todd strengthen his squad with new players for the return to the Premier League. Longer term, it was hoped the stock market listing would offer opportunities to raise even more money through rights issues.

However, the construction of the Reebok had cost around £6 million more than the original budget because of a late decision to complete the East Stand and take advantage

of the side's promotion to the Premier League. The budget spiralled from just over £25 million to closer to £32 million. At the same time, the planned sale of Burnden Park to a major supermarket, which would have gone a long way to completely financing the project, stalled. Yet much of the Mosaic money was spent on the team. None of this seemed to be to overly troubling in the summer of 1997.

Before a ball was kicked in anger, Andrew Dean, Wanderers Promotions Manager, was part of the advance party at the club's new home.

'A week or so prior to the Everton game, we moved up from Burnden, but the place was just a shell,' says Dean, a club stalwart, whose family has a long association with Wanderers. His grandfather was at the 1923 'White Horse' FA Cup Final and his great-grandfather was a Bolton councillor when the club moved from Pikes Lane to Burnden Park in 1895.

'When we got to the Reebok, I remember looking round thinking it's never going to be finished in time. We'd brought all our stuff up in boxes, and they were piled up everywhere.'

If the staff were having to cope with the upheaval of the move, the players were desperate to sample a Reebok matchday.

'We simply couldn't wait to get into the new ground and play,' recalls Taggart. 'Because the final touches to the stadium hadn't quite been made we had to play the first three games that season away from home. But the week before the game, the players were given a tour of the new ground, and we had a few night-time training sessions there to get used to the pitch and the surroundings. It was the first time I had seen the pitch close up, and to be honest we were just itching to get in the place. Pre-season was an exciting time because the lads were really buzzing, and having a new stadium to move to just added to the sense of anticipation for the new season. It was a real 21st-century set-up. Although we had enjoyed some great days at Burnden Park, the old ground was essentially a 19th-century relic. The new facilities for the players at the Reebok were absolutely brilliant. Everything about it was superb. The warm-up gym, the changing rooms, everything. The whole place was all geared up for success.'

Taggart remembers that the squad assembled by Todd went into the campaign knowing they would have to battle to achieve survival in the Premier League but full of hope they had the talent to achieve it.

'We had run away with the Division One title and we were full of confidence. The club had been relegated after just one season the last time they had been in the Premier League, but this time we all honestly felt we had a good chance of staying up. We had learnt our lessons from the season before, and we had got a few new faces in to give the squad a bit more depth. The likes of Peter Beardsley (from Newcastle United), Mark Fish (from Lazio) and Robbie Elliott (who signed for a then record £2.5 million from Newcastle) all came into the club. So we were all pretty confident, particularly having won the League so convincingly.'

That confidence was given an extra shot when, on the opening day of the season, a first-half Nathan Blake goal was enough to earn a win at Southampton. The Welsh striker then bagged two more as Wanderers fought back from 2–0 down at Coventry City to earn a point. The first defeat came at Barnsley where Bolton lost 2–1, in spite of Beardsley's first goal for the club.

So after weeks of mounting anticipation in the town, Monday 1 September 1997 arrived and the Reebok was finally open for business. Now, at last, for thousands of Wanderers supporters it was party time. Naturally Sky had brought their cameras along, and for many neutrals the stadium was as big a talking point as Todd's team. Wanderers were about to find out if concrete and steel could inspire great deeds of sporting heroism.

'We had done okay in those first three games. To pick up four points in three games away from home in the Premier League wasn't a bad effort. Now it was time for our

Summer signing: Peter Beardsley.

first game in the Reebok, and we went into the Everton game pretty confident that we could do something. As far as the players were concerned, the new stadium was never really a distraction. Before the kick-off I remember that the dressing room was a very calm place. There were a lot of good characters in there, experienced players who knew what to expect. Colin Todd also has to take a lot of credit for that because, in spite of the hype and the build-up to the game, he ensured it was a very relaxed environment. Colin always tried to make sure we played good football, and that's all he was worried about that night.'

It was a massive night in Wanderers' history, but on a wider perspective the opening of the stadium was overshadowed by the shocking death of Diana, the Princess of Wales, who had been killed in a traffic accident in Paris the day before. Naturally, the game was preceded by a minute's silence to honour her memory. It was a poignant moment as this was the first major sporting event to take place since her death.

When play got started, despite Taggart's assertions, Wanderers seemed a little overawed by the occasion. Everton created most of the early chances and Gary Speed, who would come to know the place better than most, came as close as anyone to grabbing the first goal at the Reebok – in the blue shirt of the Merseysiders. But as the night wore on Bolton finally settled into the match and their new home. Wanderers started the second half in a much more positive frame, and Neville Southall in the Everton goal was forced into making saves from Alan Thompson and then Blake.

Then, on 50 minutes, it happened. Taggart 'scored'. He had jumped to meet the ball with his head. It was meant to be a powerful effort, but he mistimed it and it turned out to be a wrong-footing header. The ball arced slow-motion style goalwards into the far corner, and a desperate Southall failed to get it. As the ball bounced down and into the net, it was hooked clear by Terry Phelan. Taggart wheeled away to celebrate, and his Bolton teammates appealed, but Barnsley referee Stephen Lodge ignored them. He waved play on. The scoreboard never flickered.

Television replays confirmed what most in the stadium suspected: the ball was six inches over the line.

'To this day, I have never seen the incident

on television or video, but I can still remember it,' says the defender. 'As the ball was crossed into the box, I challenged for it. It wasn't a clean header, but the ball looped towards the goal. Because of the way I had landed, I lost sight of it, but it appeared to go over the line. What I did see, and remember distinctly, was all the lads shouting "goal" and hands going in the air to claim it.

'But the referee just carried on. It wasn't given, so we just had to play on as if nothing

Nearly man: Gerry Taggart.

had happened. And I suppose nothing did. Of course, we didn't realise at the time that it would come back to haunt us the way it did.'

Taggart's central-defensive partner, Gudni Bergsson, also remembers the night well. 'We knew it was a big occasion for the club, and it was exciting. One thing that sticks in my mind is that we never posed for a team photo before the kick-off. Colin Todd was very superstitious and thought it might bring bad luck – he didn't want anything to spoil it. With hindsight, it's a pity because it would have been nice to have a reminder of the occasion. There was a lot riding on the game because we were back in the Premier League, Sky cameras were there, and we dearly wanted to get those three points. We should have, perhaps; Gerry's goal was clearly over the line. The result was disappointing.'

To make matters worse, new signing Elliott suffered a sickening double break to his leg – an injury so severe that it ended his season there and then – and suddenly the optimism around the Reebok, so abundant a couple of hours earlier, had taken a massive hit.

Elsewhere in the stadium, Andrew Dean's staff were still finding their feet in their new home. As part of his duties he had put

Flashpoint: Bolton and Manchester United players confront one another as Nathan Blake and United's Gary Pallister are sent off.

On target: Alan Thompson nets the first goal at the Reebok with a strike from the penalty spot against Spurs.

together the matchday programme along with secretary Simon Marland. 'For the Everton game we produced a special souvenir programme, but on the day of the game itself we didn't actually have a programme office,' says Dean. 'Everything was a bit rushed – there were even some areas of the concourse where the tarmac was only laid hours before the game! The programme was a sell-out, but because we didn't have a programme office we used the floor of the Ladies' toilets in the East Stand 10 minutes after kick-off to count the money from the sales. We felt the Ladies' would be safer than the Gents' – but it meant that any time someone wanted to use the loo, we had to pick up the cash and leave!'

Of course, the 0–0 draw against Everton was hardly a cause for panic, but the false start that it represented appeared to weigh heavy over the following few weeks. A win would have given Todd's men a certain amount of momentum and stopped any talk of a new home hoodoo from developing. It would have given the team a lift up the League table, and it would have eased some of the pressure that was already starting to build up.

As if to emphasise the importance of every point gained, Manchester United were the next visitors to the Reebok. The local rivals were greeted by a chorus of boos from three sides of the ground, United's Garry Pallister and Nathan Blake were both sent off – but the result was the same, 0–0.

In fact, fans had to wait until the visit of Spurs later that month before they saw the first goal at the Reebok. It came for Wanderers from the penalty spot off the boot of Alan Thompson. It looked as though it may be the catalyst for that elusive first victory, but a Chris Armstrong goal for Tottenham, deep into the second period, meant that for a third successive game the Reebok had yielded just a point to the hosts. The settling-in period was taking time, and Todd was also having to deal with injuries to his side.

'One of the things about the new ground was that the pitch was very hard and we suffered a lot of injuries. We'd been training on the pitch and several players picked up calf and hernia injuries because of the surface.'

October arrived with Wanderers still looking to get off the mark at their new stadium. By now tongues were wagging, and wags in the Press box were talking up the curse of the Reebok. The game against Aston Villa provided another talking point – an on-field scrap between Villa's Stan Collymore and Andy Todd, the son of the Bolton boss. Rather than the usual push and shove that football fracas are made of, this was a far more robust toe-to-toe bout with fierce punches traded. The football, however, was less memorable, with Wanderers sinking to their first defeat at the Reebok. It was a defeat which left Todd's men uncomfortably placed at the wrong end of the table and, hoodoo or no hoodoo, just three points from the first four home games told its own story.

Victory: Striker Dean Holdsworth salutes the crowd at the final whistle against Chelsea after scoring the only goal in Bolton's first League win at the Reebok.

Six long weeks after the Reebok had opened Bolton finally achieved their first win there. It came in a League Cup game against Wimbledon that was watched by a crowd of just 9,875. And even then it took extra-time to settle the encounter in Bolton's favour.

Thankfully, the first Premier League win at the Reebok soon followed. It came on 26 October 1997 against Ruud Gullit's Chelsea. Wanderers newest signing, striker Dean Holdsworth, who had arrived for a club record £3.5 million from Wimbledon, smashed home the only goal of the game. That victory, as unexpected as it was welcome, was enough to take the side out of the bottom three. When it was then quickly followed up with wins over Wimbledon and Newcastle United, Todd's side had managed to climb back towards mid-table security.

At this stage, with Christmas approaching, there was a growing feeling that the side was perhaps beginning to come to terms with both the Premier League and their new surroundings. However, that 1–0 victory over Newcastle was to be the season's high water mark. After that they found wins and points hard to come by. Either side of Christmas, Wanderers' season took shape –

Going with the Flo: defender Mark Fish, signed from Lazio, pictured challenging Tore Andre Flo of Chelsea, was a crowd favourite.

unfortunately, it was the shape of a popped party balloon, shrivelled and deflated.

The nadir was a 5–1 drubbing at home to Coventry in January. As Dion Dublin plundered goals for the Sky Blues, the rush to the Reebok exit became a stampede. It was the kind of performance that invited the tag 'relegation certainties', and yet just a week later Wanderers managed to put in a battling display and deservedly earn a 1–1 draw at Old Trafford against Manchester United. Bob Taylor, who had joined mid-season on loan from West Brom, ensured lifelong cult status among Bolton fans with the goal at Old Trafford.

Blake's heaven: Nathan Blake celebrates after scoring a late equaliser against Liverpool.

Fight back: Nathan Blake fires home as Bolton come from 3–1 down to draw 3–3 against Derby County in December.

If that result helped preserve local pride, it also underlined the Jekyll and Hyde nature of the team. The side's inconsistency, though a source of intense frustration, did keep the season interesting. Just as things looked at their bleakest, Bolton would deliver an unexpected treat and the hope was renewed.

That said, the spectre of relegation was never far away, even though Todd, at press conference after press conference, appeared as unflustered and confident as ever.

Away from home, the side had struggled, which wasn't too surprising. Their undoing was the home results. Too many drawn games

at the Reebok ensured the Wanderers were always in the mire.

Despite the relentlessly positive message from players and the management that the side would avoid the drop, finding hard evidence to support their claims was difficult. Away from home, Todd's men had been afflicted by a collective travel sickness that was so deep and long-lasting that it defied any efforts to find a cure. The side's win at Southampton on the opening day of the season had been seen as a sign of great things back in August, but going into the final three games it remained the solitary success on their travels. With two of their three remaining games away from the Reebok, the chances of a late reprieve looked slimmer than a Milan catwalk model.

However, on 25 April 1998 Todd's men went to Aston Villa and won 3–1, with goals from Neil Cox, Bob Taylor and Nathan Blake. It was Bolton's first win at Villa Park for 43 years. More importantly, it was a precious lifeline which managed to send a surge of belief to the many of the faithful.

In the weeks beforehand Todd had switched formations from 4–4–2 to three central-defenders, which seemed to have a mobilising effect on the team, but as Bolton's May date with destiny loomed something else contributed to a late rally: the Fan Factor.

Inspired by the curious mix of gallows humour and stubborn faith that are among the essential qualities of most seasoned Wanderers fans, the supporters adopted the theme from *The Great Escape* as their rallying call.

The win at Villa meant that victory in the last home game against an already doomed Crystal Palace would give Wanderers a chance of staying up. It would leave them with their fate in their own hands. Not bad for a side

Pressure point: boss Colin Todd has plenty on his mind as he watches his side suffer a 4–0 defeat at Derby in April.

that had rarely been out of the bottom three since January.

All of a sudden survival was tantalisingly within reach.

That final home game was easily the most extraordinary of that entire campaign, not least for the Reebok atmosphere. Wanderers went all out for the victory they needed, and inside 10 minutes Blake had appeared to settle the nerves with Bolton's first goal. But Palace responded almost immediately with two goals of their own, to race into a 2–1 lead. A defeat would have meant almost certain calamity for Wanderers. But this was no ordinary game. Mark Fish levelled, then Jimmy Phillips scored the goal of the game with a thumping volley, after great work from Per Frandsen, to give Bolton a 3–2 lead. All this drama came before the half-time whistle. By the break, the Reebok was absolutely buzzing. In the second half, goals from Alan Thompson and Dean Holdsworth, just his third goal of the season, put the result beyond doubt.

At the final whistle, Wanderers were celebrating a 5–2 victory. From the Nat Lofthouse Stand *The Great Escape* was bellowed with gusto, while Wanderers and Palace fans swapped shirts.

After months of playing amid the fear and dread of the drop, there was an explosion of joy at the Reebok. It was an atmosphere more akin to the opening game against Everton, but this time the result was just what was needed. It was almost surreal. The festivities were clearly the result of months of pent-up frustration. For a few brief minutes – the team did a lap of honour to acknowledge the supporters – the reality of the situation was forgotten. For a nano-second it felt as though Wanderers had survived.

In actual fact, the job was only half done. Wanderers may have reached 40 points, the Premier League's magical survival touchstone, but in May 1998 that might not be enough to avoid the drop.

A day after the Palace game, Everton were,

Crystal clear: Jimmy Phillips scores a belter as Bolton give themselves hope of avoiding relegation with a 5–2 win over Crystal Palace at the Reebok.

as expected, hammered 4–0 by champions Arsenal. So with one game left, Everton were a point behind the Wanderers, though crucially their goal difference was three better than Bolton's. All of which meant that on the final day of the season Todd's men had to travel to Chelsea and match Everton's result at home to Coventry at Goodison Park.

Despite the acclaim that greeted the 5–2 win over Palace, that final game at Stamford Bridge turned out to be a game too far for Todd's weary troops. As expected, Wanderers threw everything they had at Chelsea early on, and even when news that Everton had taken an early lead at Goodison filtered through it failed to quell the jollity among Wanderers' travelling fans.

Per Frandsen thought he had given the side a precious first-half lead when he went on a 70-yard run through the middle of Chelsea's star-studded team. It was a fantastic effort that left the celebrated pair of Frank Leboeuf and Laurent Charvet bamboozled. Having created the opening, Frandsen kept his nerve to steer the ball past Ed De Goey in the Chelsea goal. Wanderers fans were on their feet, waiting to celebrate a goal of the season contender. But, as the ball trickled towards the net, Chelsea's Dennis Wise raced back and hoofed it clear. The thwarted Dane remembers the incident with his usual understatement. 'We went into the game with lots of hope and we had our chances. I had one in the first half when I went on a run, but Dennis Wise stopped it on the line.'

It was a gut-wrenching moment. Instead of leaping in celebration, Todd beat a rhythm of frustration on the dug-out roof. 'We played pretty well that day and had our chances, but I think the difference between the two teams was in their subs bench. They had some quality internationals there,' says Todd.

So it proved. With the score 0–0 at half-time, Chelsea player-boss Gianluca Vialli brought himself, Gustavo Poyet and Roberto Di Matteo on to freshen up the home side, and on 73 minutes Vialli broke the deadlock.

Bolton, already wearied by their first-half efforts in the West London heat, appeared shattered. They were urged forward to cries of 'Attack, attack, attack!' which increased in fervour after news that Coventry had levelled at Everton. The players had an entire season weighing on them and it showed. For weeks they had defied expectations, but at the very last they were unable to rally for one final time.

So close: Per Frandsen is denied by Dennis Wise as he comes close to giving Bolton the lead at Chelsea on the final day of the season.

Feeling down: Bolton 'keeper Keith Branagan slumps as the final whistle sounds at Stamford Bridge.

The game was up when Jody Morris scored just before the final whistle, though, just to add a touch of the bizarre to a day of paralysing tension, some Chelsea fans booed their own side's goals – seemingly preferring to see Everton go down.

Frandsen adds 'We heard the Bolton fans cheer when Coventry equalised at Everton, which meant that if we could score we would stay up, but we couldn't manage it. They scored again and we went down on goal difference – it was a major disappointment.'

With relegation confirmed, the inquest started, and as Everton were the beneficiaries of that last-day drama all Wanderers supporters' thoughts drifted back to that Reebok curtain raiser and the Gerry Taggart 'goal'.

For Todd it was simple: 'The ball crossed the line. As things panned out, that robbed us that season. We should have stayed up. In football you always need that little bit of luck, and on that occasion we didn't get it. A win against Everton would have given us an extra two points, but in the end we went down with 40 points on goal difference.'

Says Bergsson, 'Going down on the final day of the season was absolutely shattering for the side. Looking back, I still believe we had the team and the personnel to stay up, but it just wasn't to be.'

However, not everyone buys into the bad luck theory. Striker Dean Holdsworth had been signed to deliver the goals to help keep the side up. Instead, he endured a miserable first season at the club and believes the team's unhappy fate is straightforward to analyse.

'There was no lack of effort from any of the players and no lack of belief that we could survive, but the Premier League is a very tough place to play, and over a season you find out whether you're good enough. I don't

think we were,' he says. 'You can say that we were unlucky here or had a bad break there, but I don't think the table lies at the end of a season. We battled and the supporters were great to the side. There was a real Cup Final atmosphere against Crystal Palace in particular. Winning that day gave us a chance, but in the end it wasn't enough.

'It was a fantastic stadium, but we were struggling on the park. I remember the very first time that I drove down the M61 and saw the stadium from a distance; it made the hairs on the back of my neck stand up. I knew straight away on seeing it that it would be a fantastic place to play football. On reflection, a lot of money was spent on the stadium. I think that obviously affected the team on the pitch. That said, it was a fantastic decision to build the stadium because it eventually enabled the club to flourish when we got back into the Premier League again.

'But that first season was a learning process for the club, and in the end I guess we found that the squad just wasn't good enough. It was a really tough time for all the players. When you're in a relegation struggle like that, it is very hard to keep your spirits up, and, although the stadium was great, the training facilities at that point weren't up to much. It was nobody's fault particularly. In some ways the club had gone too far, too quickly.'

I guess the final word on the Reebok's first season should go to Taggart. For him, the campaign was a hugely frustrating one, as injury added to the insult of the Everton match. He was sidelined for several months with an ankle ligament strain and only

Despair: a young fan is comforted as Bolton's relegation is confirmed.

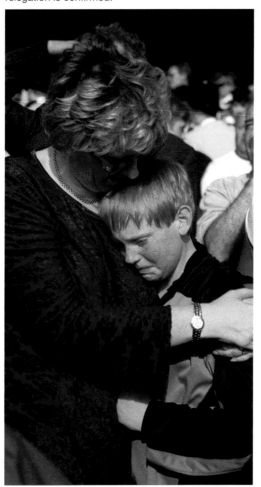

returned to the first team just in time to play his part in the heart-breaking climax for Bolton – against Villa, Palace and Chelsea.

'The place was really buzzing after the win against Palace. It was a great match and a great atmosphere. When we went to Chelsea, we knew there was a lot at stake, but we also knew we had our fate in our hands.

'My feeling is that nerves got to us in the end. I can still see Per Frandsen's chance early on and if that had gone in it might have settled us. It was a baking hot day and we put so much effort in early into the match that we just physically ran out of steam. We were really deflated when the first Chelsea goal went in and the second was just a formality.'

From a distance of 10 years, Taggart is still aggrieved by the opening-night howler.

'I have been asked lots of times since "Would we have stayed up if the goal against Everton had gone in?" And to my mind, the answer is "Yes." I think so, I really do.

'I think that a win against Everton would have meant more than the three points. A victory would have given us the lift and the impetus we needed. We would have had something to build on. Instead, we took a long time to settle. It took weeks for us to get our first win at the Reebok and the pressure started to increase as the games went by. The stadium became a monkey on our backs. We would have avoided all of that nonsense with a win over Everton that night – and in my mind, we really should have won it.'

The defeat at Chelsea turned out to be Taggart's last game in a Bolton shirt. He joined Leicester City that summer.

'I would have stayed if we had survived because I really enjoyed my three years at Bolton. My first season at the club was a disaster because of injuries. The second was superb when we won the League. And the third was, again, stop-start. I thought I played well but couldn't seem to shake off the injuries. They had a big bearing on my three seasons, and, if I could have stayed fit, who knows? Maybe that would have been the difference between us staying up and going down.'

1997–98 was a season of maybes.

On reflection, the one thing you can say with certainty is that the first season at the Reebok highlighted one of football's oldest chestnuts. There's a fine line between success and failure – it's a mere six inches.

Reebok firsts

1. Game: against Everton in the Premier League, 1 September 1997
2. Goal: Alan Thompson against Spurs, 23 September 1997
3. Red card(s): Nathan Blake and Gary Pallister (Man United), 20 September 1997
4. Bolton win: 3-0 against Wimbledon in the League Cup
5. League victory: 1-0 against Chelsea, 26 October 1997
6. Defeat: 1-0 against Aston Villa, 4 October 1997
7. Hat-trick: Dean Holdsworth against Scunthorpe in the FA Cup, 28 January 2001
8. Outfield player to play in goal: Bo Hansen against Newcastle United, October 2001
9. European game: against Lokomotiv Plovdiv,15 September 2005
10. Bolton player to score in Europe: El-Hadji Diouf, 15 September 2005

1997–98

Ins

Hasney Aljofree (trainee), Neil Cox (Middlesbrough), Arnar Gunnlaugsson (Akranes), Robbie Elliott (Newcastle), Dean Holdsworth (Wimbledon), Mike Whitlow (Leicester City), Bob Taylor (West Bromwich Albion), Mark Fish (Lazio), Franz Carr (loan, Nottingham Forest), Dean Holden (trainee), John Salako (Coventry City).

Outs

John McGinlay (Bradford City), Scott McAnespie (Fulham), Franz Carr (Nottingham Forest), Jamie Pollock (Manchester City).

The Watford Gap

Movie stars. Forget 'em. Who needs Hollywood when you've got the Premier League? For the best part of a century football had rarely ventured off the back pages, except to record the odd riot or bedroom and taproom exploits of a fallen idol or two. In the 60s, 70s and even into the 80s live matches on TV were sacred communal events – keenly anticipated simply because of their rarity. Then in the 1990s all that changed. Football became a fashion accessory. As the bard might have put it, suddenly all the world was a football pitch and the players simply gods. When David Beckham shaved his head, there were queues around the block at barbers from Breightmet to Burma. Football had all the attributes that the media prized: well-toned athletes, thrilling sporting encounters, glamour and, thanks to the Sky television contracts, huge wealth. Well, at the very top it did. What the establishment of the Premier League also created was a Grand Canyon-sized gap between the elite and the also-rans.

So, after a season at the top table, relegation meant that Bolton swapped life in the fast lane for life in the bus lane. Or, to put it another way, in 1997 the season's opener at the Reebok pitched Bolton against Everton, 12 months later Grimsby Town were the visitors, and, before you ask, no, Sky didn't show it live.

Leader: Gudni Bergsson

Vision: Bolton boss Colin Todd, who spent his Sundays overseas scouting for new talent.

Gudni Bergsson remembers the contrast vividly. 'It was difficult at first to get used to that. The stadium wasn't full like it had been in the first year, and it was very obvious at the Reebok. The crowds went from full houses to something nearer the 17,000-mark, so there were a lot of empty seats. 17,000 would have looked a reasonable crowd at Burnden Park and you probably wouldn't have been so aware of all the gaps.'

It was like going cold turkey, and Wanderers desperately needed another Premier League fix. The urgency wasn't simply fuelled by desire to restore battered pride or professional status. The club needed the money. The balance sheet had been given a little boost thanks to a parachute payment from their TV paymasters but, having invested so heavily in the Reebok stadium and the side 12 months earlier, the pressure was now on Colin Todd and his team to make an immediate return to the big League of packed houses and TV millions.

While building the Reebok a decision had been taken by the board to increase the spending, taking the budget of £25 million to more than £30 million, as a decision was taken to complete the East Stand. At the same time, after getting promotion, Todd had been given free rein with the chequebook and millions more had gone on transfer fees and wages for players in a bid to secure Premier League football. Given

New face: chief executive Allan Duckworth, who was brought to the club by Phil Gartside.

Wanderers' relatively limited means, it had been a risky strategy based on hopes of full houses and the sale of Burnden Park. By September 1998 both ideas were looking optimistic.

So, if the mood on the terraces was subdued, it was anything but in the boardroom. Tensions were growing. The sale of Burnden was a key plank in the strategy that (alongside grants) would help finance the move to Middlebrook. But at this stage it still hadn't happened. The future was uncertain but one thing was clear: Division One football wasn't going to ease the huge financial burden created by developing a Premier League set-up. It was a case of trying to stave off creditors long enough for Colin Todd to engineer a Premier League return.

At this point the board turned to Allan Duckworth – financial director of Umbro. He was approached by director Phil Gartside and initially spurned his advances to get involved in the club. 'When I first spoke to him, I told him I wasn't interested,' says Duckworth. 'But Phil is a very persuasive guy, and when we met up I found it was a real meeting of minds. I immediately got on with him, and Phil already had a vision that the Reebok was going to be more than a football club. He knew the club had to do something. What they really needed was somebody who could help them devise a strategy. I felt then that an opportunity like that doesn't come along very often. Even so, it was more a case of me joining Phil Gartside than me joining Bolton

Wanderers to be honest. Then I met the chairman Gordon Hargreaves. It was Gordon's vision that got the stadium project going in the first place. He had the vision to see that Bolton needed a new home, he knew the town very well and, fortunately, he also had the vision to see that this land, which was a patch of peat bog, could become a football stadium. A lot of that initial conceptual thinking was Gordon Hargreaves, so I've a lot of time for Gordon.

'I was coming in at a very base level – it was almost as though I had a blank piece of paper, because when I first got here there was no clear sign of a strategy. They had a fantastic stadium, nobody could dispute that, but I just don't think they had sat down and worked out how they were going to turn the vision into a reality. No one had worked out how they were going to run it and make a profit or at least break even. The thinking appeared to have ended at the conceptual design stage and maybe they had been carried away a little bit with 'the project'.

'It's easy talking with hindsight, but I think the club lacked a hard-nosed project team to make sure we cut our cloth to fit. I don't think anybody was overseeing the project in terms of being really tight on costs and realising that the design had to be shrunk down. The stadium was all built for comfort and luxury. It was a statement being made and it's a lovely statement, but it's an expensive one!'

Excited by the challenge, Duckworth was convinced that he could work with Gartside and Hargreaves, but his initial assessment of the club's financial state was that things were even worse than he'd thought.

'I had a good idea of what the issues were, but then I found out that there were players that had been bought who still hadn't been paid for. So, the debt was going to grow before it came down. At the time the debt was about £30 million. We were a loss-making club with a stadium that was a shell in most areas and incapable of earning money. We also had a newly-relegated team. Yet just to keep the stadium going was going to cost us circa £1 million a year. The first task was to stabilise the debt and get the confidence of the bank, because the big issue was that the bank had lost confidence – they obviously felt that the whole thing was going out of control. Phil knew this and bringing me in helped the club buy time with the bank.'

So, Gartside and Duckworth set to work on putting together a very basic business plan to help keep the bank happy.

Despite relegation, the club kept faith with Todd, and he started his own planning. His aim was simple – to engineer an early return to the Premier League. But by this time his spending power was substantially reduced. One of the side-effects of the blanket TV coverage was that football now enjoyed the arrival of the foreign legion.

What had started as a trickle in the previous decade had turned into a torrent by 1998. The dressing rooms of most leading clubs now rang with the chatter of more foreign accents than the Heathrow arrivals hall, and Wanderers were no different. In order to compete in what was rapidly turning into a global game, Todd had taken the decision early in his tenure as Bolton boss to have a more European focus when it came to trying to find new talent. But, rather than the mature markets in Italy, Spain, Germany and France, where prices were spiralling, Todd turned his attentions to Scandinavia. Within days of taking over as manager he was studying flight schedules for unpro-nounceable far-flung destinations and

investing in thermals and fleeces. Sundays may have been a day of rest for most, but for Todd they were made for scouting missions.

'I decided very early on to look towards Scandinavian players, and I used to go on regular scouting trips there. I would go across on Sunday mornings and whenever it was possible I'd try to take in two games. I wanted to see as many players as possible.'

The first fruits of Todd's Sunday shopping sprees arrived in pre-Reebok days. Following Wanderers' relegation from the Premier League in 1996, Danes Per Frandsen and Michael 'Smurf' Johansen were signed from FC Copenhagen for £2.25 million, which represented incredibly good value at the time. Frandsen turned up at Burnden Park with three caps for his country to his name and a reputation for collecting yellow cards. Small and red-haired, Johansen was immediately compared to Gordon Strachan, but more for his ability on the ball rather than his physical attributes. Both made an immediate impact in Wanderers' Championship-winning side of 1996.

Says Todd, 'I had looked at one game and stayed for about 20 minutes because the lad I'd gone out there to see wasn't playing and no one else caught my eye. So I went across to another game in Copenhagen, which was only about 15 minutes away. I managed to see the whole second half, and that's when I first saw Per Frandsen and Michael Johansen playing. I watched them a couple of times more before deciding to bring them in. Per was the one who caught my eye first. At that time he was something of a journeyman footballer, but he was an experienced guy and had a good football brain. He was strong, and I knew straight away that the pair of them would be alright in English football. Mind you, neither Per nor Michael had ever really done the type of pre-season training we were used to, and to be honest I think it really took it out of them. They both started that first season well but faded. I think by Christmas they were absolutely goosed. They needed to adapt and that was the one thing they had to improve on.'

When the Danes arrived at Bolton there were already a couple of Scandinavians in the camp: Finnish striker Mixu Paatelainen and defender Gudni Bergsson from Iceland. The latter had arrived from Reykjavik via London a year earlier than Frandsen and Johansen. Between 1988 and 1995 Bergsson had made

72 rather sporadic appearances for Tottenham Hotspur but was allowed to join Wanderers for just £65,000 in the spring of 1995, after being told he was surplus to requirements at White Hart Lane. He actually made his Wanderers debut at Wembley as a substitute in the League Cup Final defeat against Liverpool. A few short weeks later, he was back at the Twin Towers playing his part in the breathless 4–3 Play-off Final win over Reading. During that era the bulk of the 'foreign' accents in the Bolton dressing room tended to belong to the Scottish and Irish contingent, but the team easy assimilated the likes of Gudni and convinced the coaching staff to look further afield.

Spurred on by his success with Frandsen and Johansen, Todd stepped up his Sunday scouting missions. Icelandic forward Arnar Gunnlaugsson arrived in 1997 and went on to make a handful of Premier League appearances during that ill-fated 'goal that never was' campaign. A young goalkeeper, Jussi Jaaskelainen, also arrived in November 1997. Todd paid a reported £300,000 for Jussi, who has gone on to play more than 350 games for the club. Not a bad investment.

Relegation meant the pack had to be

Sublime: Bolton substitute Arnar Gunnlaugsson scores a last-minute equaliser to earn his side a point on the opening day of the season.

shuffled once more, and with the likes of Gerry Taggart, Alan Thompson, Peter Beardsley and others all departing Todd needed to bring in new faces. Once again he turned to his favourite hunting ground, Scandinavia. He recruited Claus Jensen, then a fresh-faced Danish Under-21 midfielder. The latter's capture showed the value of Todd's missions.

'I used to enjoy the Scandinavian scouting trips, and I actually made a point of doing them myself, which is how I ended up spotting Jussi. I wasn't actually looking for him specifically, I'd gone across to Finland to take in the senior international match

between Finland and Norway, but on the Tuesday night beforehand there was an Under-21 game. I decided to take a look at that one too, and I'm really glad I did. Jussi was in goal for the young Finland side, and I remember being so impressed that while I was at the match I rang Gordon Hargreaves and told him I had spotted a new goalkeeper. He told me there and then to pursue it. However, there was a bit of a mix-up about who Jussi's agent was, and by the time I had managed to get that sorted he was having a trial with Norwich City. We managed to snatch him from under their noses, and we signed him for £300,000. I was pleased with that one, but there were several others who came in. A lot of good footballers signed for me during that time.'

In the summer of 1998 Todd unearthed another diamond from the frozen north. This one would give the Bolton forward line more sparkle.

'During our pre-season tour in Dublin I got a call about a young lad who had been playing at PSV in Holland. He had suffered a serious injury and had been told by doctors that he was unlikely to play again. So the lad had gone back to his native Iceland where he'd been told it would be difficult to get back into the game because of the injuries he'd had. But he had worked extremely hard to try and get his fitness back so we invited him over to Ireland to have a look at him. When he turned up the lad was really out of shape and overweight. I was a bit taken aback, he must have been two stone overweight at least, but as soon as we saw him on the pitch we saw what skill he had, and we knew that we had to sign him.'

The youngster in question was one Eidur Gudjohnsen. He was still only 19 and had

Playing safe: Finnish 'keeper Jussi Jaaskelainen during his Bolton debut at Crystal Palace.

played at PSV with Ronaldo before a serious ankle injury he collected playing for his national Under-21 side, ironically in Dublin, threatened to bring his career to a premature end. Even despite the medical concerns and his lack of overall fitness, Todd backed his judgement in just one quick viewing. He said 'Given his CV, having played at one of the biggest clubs in Europe, it was something of a coup getting him to the club.'

Todd's right-hand man Phil Brown agrees: 'I'll never forget the first time we saw Eidur play. Colin and I were stood on the touchline in Dublin watching him and at the same instant we turned to one another and nodded. Nothing was said. The nod was all it needed. It was one of those moments where you just knew…

'Eidur was an exceptional talent. When he came to Bolton he was overweight because of his injuries and his lack of fitness, but he had great touch and fantastic awareness. Eidur had that special ability to see the final pass like Paul Scholes or Peter Beardsley. He could play in that role just behind the main striker and, on top of that, he was a goalscorer as well. I think we paid just over £100,000 for him and eventually sold him for more than £4 million. But on that trip to Ireland all you could see was an awful lot of potential.

'We knew he would have no problem fitting in because by then Scandinavia had become a real hotbed for us. After we had taken Per and Michael we realised that it was a good market for us. They had fitted in well, both technically and mentally, and they were excellent players. The mentality in that region was similar to the English mentality, the climate was similar too and they understood the game. We viewed it as a really good market, and, just as importantly, it was good value. Players from that neck of the woods were a lot cheaper, say, than in France or Italy where the market had just gone sky high.

'Michael Johansen wasn't an out and out winger. Though he played wide on the right he had a tendency to come inside. He didn't have the out and out pace of an orthodox winger so he adapted his game and played a position halfway between an inside right and an outside right. We also brought in Claus Jensen. Claus was an intelligent footballer with great touch and great ability.'

Having assembled their smorgasbord of Scandinavian talent, Todd and Brown set about trying to win back a place at the top table.

For a young man like Jensen the move to Bolton couldn't have been easier. 'When I arrived here there was already a strong Danish contingent with Per and Michael Johansen already at the club, and later that

Dane again: Claus Jensen boosted the Danish contingent at the Reebok after his arrival in the summer of 1998.

season Bo Hansen joined from Brondby. It was easy for me to settle in. I remember speaking to Per just before I came to the club, and he had only good things to say about the club, but certainly it helped me at the start of my career in England to have players around me that I could talk to. But it wasn't just my fellow Danes, I have to say all the players helped me fit in.'

If Jensen had any doubts about the club then the Reebok factor helped to dispel them: 'The day I arrived in Bolton I was put up in a hotel right opposite the ground, and I had a

view of the Reebok. Being able to see the stadium from the hotel room made signing for the club a very easy decision. And because Per and Michael were already here I already knew that Bolton was a fantastic club, and I was really excited to be joining. Colin Todd told me that I was going to be a big part of his plans and that he really believed in me.'

By now the undisputed king of the Reebok was the thinking fan's blond bombshell Per Frandsen. The Copenhagen man had come agonisingly close to scoring the goal that might have helped preserve their Premier League status at Chelsea on the final day of the previous season.

When Wanderers started the 1998–99 season he appeared determined to take the side back, single-handed if he had to. The central-midfield man swiftly became the heartbeat of Todd's newly-fashioned team. Hugely determined, he could pick out a pass with laser-like accuracy and his Thor hammer of a shot carried enough force to crack open the tightest of defences. Allied to such technical gifts, Frandsen possessed an intelligence and ability to read the game. If any one player personified Todd's playing style it was Frandsen. He used the ball cleverly, orchestrated attacking moves and always looked to create something.

Not surprisingly Frandsen has fond memories of that season. 'At that time we really had a great side. We had lost a few players but managed to keep hold of people like Mark Fish and Gudni Bergsson. We had also brought in some quality players like Claus Jensen, Jussi and Ricardo Gardner. With Claus, Smurf (Michael Johansson) and later Bo Hansen we had four Danish players in the side. We played some really excellent football that season and I really enjoyed playing in that team. It was very much in Colin Todd's style. Smurf and I had been at the club for a while, but Claus settled in very quickly and looked at ease.'

The midfielder wasn't simply an inspiration to the team on matchdays, his influence spread throughout the club. One of his biggest fans was a young apprentice by the name of Kevin Nolan.

'As a young scholar seeing Per up close was an unbelievable treat, because I played in the same position as him,' says Nolan. 'He was always encouraging me and wanted me to do well. He used to say to me 'Kevin I don't want to be playing next to you, I want you to

playing instead of me!' He just gave me so much confidence in my own ability.

'On the pitch he was quality and that's why he became such a hero to me. Per's passing ability was fantastic, and he scored some absolute screamers. He also had a knack of scoring important goals for us. But the thing that made him different was his attitude. He was a winner. He wanted to win more than anyone I've ever met. I've probably had more fights with Per than I have with any other player simply because he wanted everyone to do the best they could and he wanted the best for Bolton Wanderers.'

The Danish quartet bonded instantly, indeed Frandsen and Jensen remain great friends. 'All of us got on well straight away,' says Jensen. 'We were friends on and off the field, and we found it really easy to adapt to life in north-west England and settle in at Bolton. The club really looked after us and we had some really good characters in the side.'

With Frandsen calling the shots, Wanderers got off to an excellent start. Gunnlaugsson, in particular, caught the eye during the opening weeks of the season. The bald-headed striker came on as a late substitute on the opening day at Crystal

Empty feeling: Neil Cox challenges for a ball with Crystal Palace's Lee Bradbury amid the Reebok's empty seats.

Palace, grabbing the last-minute equaliser that ensured Wanderers' pleasing passing performance was rewarded with a point.

Todd's men may no longer have been playing to the packed houses, but the side's blend of technically-gifted Scandinavians and British grit produced football that was very easy on the eye. The side was scoring freely and proving hard to beat. In fact, Wanderers' unbeaten start in League and Cup had stretched to an impressive 15 games until Watford, managed by former England boss Graham Taylor, won 2–1 at the Reebok on 20 October.

Trick or treat: Bolton's Danish star Michael Johansen, who was compared to Gordon Strachan.

That setback was nothing compared with the blow later that month when the club accepted an offer of £4.25 million for Welsh international striker Nathan Blake by Blackburn Rovers. Blake had been Wanderers' top scorer the season before, but the financial pressures were such and the bid so good that the club simply couldn't turn it down.

Meanwhile, not every player was taking to life in Division One as well as Frandsen. For striker Dean Holdsworth the adjustment,

after a career spent mainly in the top flight, was tough. 'Being back in Division One was not new for the club, but it was very hard to shift that feeling of disappointment. It went from the stands, where you could see row after row of empty seats, to the players. The attendances were down, the games were tough and there was constant pressure on the side to go straight back up. We knew what we had to do but it was a tough time. My philosophy is that all experiences are useful,

Brothers in arms: Bolton's Dean Holdsworth fends off twin brother David during the game against Sheffield United — the match finished 2–2.

difficult for all of us, particularly after suffering such a disappointment, getting so close to staying up and then not doing, and we started off pretty slowly, but we were professionals and we knew we had to carry on.'

but it was very hard to remain positive. As time went on, there were several changes behind the scenes in the club, and as a player you never really knew where you were at, and I found it difficult.

'I'd come from Wimbledon where team spirit was everything, and at Bolton it wasn't like that. The manager, Colin Todd, wasn't big on days out golfing and that sort of thing. He didn't see that as the way things should go. There were also a lot of Scandinavian lads who technically were excellent, but viewed the role of a footballer as a job. For me it was more than that – it is more than that. It's also about looking after your teammates.'

Bergsson too found it hard to shake off the relegation blues: 'That second season was

These contrasting views from the dressing room were mirrored in the up and down fortunes of the side. The October defeat against Watford and sale of Blake marked the beginning of a five-game sequence without a win.

But then between November and February Wanderers went on a 15-game unbeaten sequence that included a 4–0 hammering of neighbours Bury, and Reebok victories over Crystal Palace, Portsmouth, Norwich and West Brom. The latter on 13 February was the club's sixth successive win and took Wanderers up to second in the table, with the players convinced that they could still catch runaway leaders Sunderland in the race for the title.

Says Jensen, 'When I arrived at the club, even though they'd been relegated the season before, there was definitely a feeling of ambition and desire to get straight back into the Premier League. We played a passing kind of football all the way through the side from defence to attack and it was a joy to play in that side.'

When the unbeaten run came to an end it did so against rock bottom Crewe. They rolled up at the Reebok and stunned the Wanderers by winning 3–1 largely due to some suspect defending by the home team. Todd's men slipped from second to fourth, and worse was to follow later that week when more goals were shipped in a 3–2 defeat against Huddersfield. Despite a high quality midfield quartet of Scott Sellars, Frandsen, Johansen and Jensen that was the envy of most of their rivals, Wanderers went from promotion favourites to Play-off hopefuls in the space of a miserable few weeks. The team were still scoring freely but defensively there were clearly problems.

'I believed in keeping clean sheets, but also believed in playing the game with a certain amount of panache and style,' says Todd.

Victory over QPR at the Reebok in March ended a five-match winless sequence, but then the club embarked on another disappointing spell, including a 2–0 defeat at Watford who were closing in on Todd's men. By now, automatic promotion was a forlorn hope and the focus switched to Play-off qualification. Even that started to look doubtful as the poor sequence continued.

Spring brought a new lease of life. Victories over Bristol City and Ipswich and a draw at Norwich revived hopes. The bright spell coincided with the emergence of Eidur Gudjohnsen.

By now the striker was sufficiently fit to start matches, and he proved Todd and Brown's judgement was spot on. After two years on the sidelines Gudjohnsen was determined to make up for lost time. His impact was instant, and it was immediately clear that Bolton had unearthed a very special talent. He was to score five goals in 14 games that season and earned the nickname The Ice Man. His emergence came at just the right time and provided the whole squad with a much-needed lift.

However, it was still a very nervy period. An unwelcome 2–1 defeat at Bury meant Bolton could be overtaken by Wolves and

Watford in the final run-in and miss out completely on a Play-off place.

The margins were extremely tight. Ricardo Gardner scored a vital goal for Wanderers in a 1–1 draw with Wolves at the Reebok that took them back up to fifth in the table on 73 points, ahead of Watford on goals scored and one point ahead of the Molineux men.

Twelve months previously the question had been whether Bolton would avoid the drop, now it was a question of whether they would make the Play-offs, and they were

Caribbean star: summer signing Ricardo Gardner.

anxiously looking for others to do them a favour. It came when Wolves could only draw their game in hand against Grimsby.

Once again Wanderers went into the final day of the season with everything to play for. The side needed a final day win at Portsmouth to be sure of their Play-off berth. Goals from Johansen and Gudjohnsen secured the three points to set up what turned out to be an extraordinary Play-off clash with Ipswich Town.

Wanderers had won both League encounters against the Tractor Boys and took the honours in the first leg at the Reebok 1–0, thanks to a stunning goal from one of Todd's trusty Danes – the irrepressible Johansen.

What followed was an incredible second leg at Portman Road. Wanderers lost 4–3 on the night after extra-time to go through thanks to the away-goals rule. The *Bolton Evening News* reporter Gordon Sharrock, who has seen his fair share of matches, summed up the night like this: 'To call this just a football match simply doesn't do justice to the event. Those who witnessed it first hand might never be the same again. They'll certainly have every right to scoff whenever games are

Per-fect timing: Frandsen (second from right) celebrates after scoring the second Bolton goal in the Play-off thriller at Ipswich.

described as "sensational", "pulsating" or "dramatic". This wasn't just another game – it was an emotional experience.'

Matt Holland had made the aggregate scores level in the 13th minute, only for Bob Taylor to restore Wanderers' advantage five minutes into the second half. Within a minute Kieron Dyer made it 2–1 on the night and level on aggregate. Then Per Frandsen made it advantage Bolton again, scoring with just seven minutes of normal time left on the clock. However, Dyer grabbed an injury time goal to take the tie into extra-time. Six minutes into it Taylor scored again to make the aggregate score 4–3 to Bolton, and

although Holland scored again Wanderers had booked a date at Wembley where Graham Taylor's Watford were waiting.

Having come through such a testing tie against a side that had finished the League campaign 10 points ahead of Wanderers, the confidence flooded back to the Reebok. But Watford had surprised many by qualifying for the Play-off Final and had beaten Bolton twice already that season.

Unfortunately, it wasn't to be third time lucky for Bolton.

Wanderers left Wembley depressed by a 2–0 defeat and disappointed by the fact that they had failed to turn on the style they knew

Bob on: Wanderers striker Bob Taylor and manager Colin Todd celebrate after the final whistle at Ipswich.

they were capable of. But in some ways it was a display that summed up the campaign. It had promised much early on, but ultimately the team failed to deliver.

'I don't know what it was, but we just never seemed to play well against Watford that season,' says Frandsen. 'We had lost at their place in the run-in, and they had already beaten us at home. They were definitely our bogey side that year. In the Final we had some chances, but we didn't really play well.

'We knew the result of the game would have a massive effect on the club. We all knew how important it was for the side to bounce straight back to the Premier League, and we just couldn't do it. It was a major disappointment. We had come close but not close enough.'

For the second successive year, Wanderers had gone into the final game of the season knowing that a win would give them Premier League status. For the second successive season, the final game had started with high hopes. And for the second successive season the final game had ended with a horribly familiar depressing emptiness.

Says Brown, 'The defeat against Watford was very dispiriting. It was bitterly disappointing not to go up, but it was also bitterly disappointing because it was a game in which we didn't really put in a decent

Final agony: Watford 'keeper Alec Chamberlain saves from Bolton striker Eidur Gudjohnsen in the Play-off Final.

Wembley woe: Wanderers players slump to the ground after defeat against Watford.

Top 10 Goalscorers for Bolton Wanderers Football Club	
Nat Lofthouse	– 285
Joe Smith	– 277
David Jack	– 161
Jack Milsom	– 153
Ray Westwood	– 144
Willie Moir	– 134
John Byrom	– 130
Harold Blackmore	– 122
Neil Whatmore	– 121
John McGinlay	– 118

1998–99

Ins

Claus Jensen (Lyngby), Ricardo Gardner (Harbour View), Jon Newsome (loan, Sheffield Wednesday), Paul Warhurst (Crystal Palace), Bo Hansen (Brondby), Steve Banks (Blackpool), Gaetano Giallanza (loan, FC Nantes), Jussi Jaaskelainen (VPS Vaasa), Eidur Gudjohnsen (KR Reykjavik).

Outs

Gerry Taggart (Leicester City), Nathan Blake (Blackburn Rovers), Arnar Gunnlaugsson (Leicester City), Nicky Spooner (Charleston Battery), John Salako (Fulham), John Sheridan (Doncaster), Scott Taylor (Tranmere), Alan Thompson (Aston Villa), Gavin Ward (Stoke City), Gaetano Giallanza (loan, FC Nantes).

display. All your season's work goes because of one bad performance.

'It had been a transitional season, and although the financial pressures of relegation had started to bite I felt Colin Todd had bought very wisely. He had laid the foundations for future years by bringing in people like Jussi Jaaskelainen, Ricardo Gardner, Eidur Gudjohnsen and Claus Jensen.'

Brown was half right. For, while the club had a few valuable assets on the playing front, thanks to the Reebok they had a Premier League stadium and a Premier League wage bill, though were facing the prospect of another season in Division One.

Something had to give.

Chapter Three 1999–2000
The Second Coming

Some people say that a banker is the kind of guy who will lend you an umbrella when it's sunny and want it back when it starts to rain. Well, in the wake of the Play-off Final defeat against Watford at Wembley the storm clouds were massing over the Reebok.

Failure to regain Premier League status had a price. The Reebok board was now under severe pressure from the bank to explain how they would meet the club's commitments. The only assets it possessed were the ones pulling on the jerseys on a Saturday afternoon. If wolves were going to be kept from the door the choice was obvious. At a board meeting in the immediate aftermath of the Watford game, manager Colin Todd was told that his prize assets were going to have to go.

'I was always given tremendous backing by the board, and I had enjoyed an excellent relationship with the then chairman Gordon Hargreaves,' says Todd. 'The board had been very stable for a long time, but after the Play-off defeat things changed, and I could tell the writing was on the wall. The harmony had gone and there were people on the board who clearly had conflicting ideas about which direction the club should go.'

As the financial realities of another season in Division One hit home, a rift developed among the board members on exactly how to handle the problem. Two factions emerged, with Hargreaves in one corner and Phil Gartside in the other. Gartside, a board member since 1987 and an accountant by training, felt Wanderers had to face up to the fact the business plan wasn't working and radical surgery was needed.

'We had a board meeting on the Tuesday following the Play-off defeat and the accountant in me surfaced,' he says. 'I told the other directors that we had to find a way to restructure the debt before the bank came along and told us to. I really felt strongly that we had to put a new plan together that showed we were determined to get to grips with things. It was ultimatum time. We had to do it, or I was going to walk away. We also had to find some money – a lot of money – very quickly.

'At that meeting Colin Todd made it clear he didn't want to sell anybody, but unfortunately in my view we had got to the stage where we really didn't have a choice. By July the inevitable happened and the bank tapped us on the shoulder. They told us they wanted us to find some equity and to look at sorting out the debt – fast. The bank was insisting that we started to repay some debts and the only assets that we could realise were Mark Fish and Per Frandsen. We had to sell.'

With chief executive Allan Duckworth, Gartside had hatched a plan to address the situation in the long term. 'We had to sell players if necessary, anything to raise money and get the confidence of the bank,' says Duckworth. 'But actually our aim was to spend some more money to complete the development of the stadium so that we could make money. At that point we had an empty stadium though it had the infrastructure in place to develop it further.

Key mover: Per Frandsen celebrates after scoring against Birmingham, but the Dane would soon be heading for the Reebok exit.

'Our strategy was to try and develop a business that was centred on the football club but where a significant proportion of our earnings came from activities that were not directly related to football. That seemed to us to be sensible because it meant that even if we weren't in the Premier League we could pay our bills. We wouldn't be entirely dependent on football.

'The club had always planned to have a hotel at the stadium and this became our focus. Gordon Hargreaves, who used to run a hotel in the area, played a large part in that original concept. The club had already commissioned a feasibility study by Andersons Consultants through their hotel division based in London. It wanted an independent assessment of whether there was the need for a hotel in this area – they needed to know what type of hotel it ought to be, how many bedrooms, what the market was like, what the competition was like, the pricing and so on. We needed to know from the outset if the cost of building a hotel could be justified by the revenue that we would earn.'

The feedback had been positive so the board had started to look for a partner to develop the plan. The search for a partner had led them to McDonald's Hotels and De Vere Hotels.

'It quickly became apparent to us that De Vere were much closer in tune with our thinking; the standard of the hotel we were after was good. The other reason why a hotel seemed to make sense was because the stadium had already been built with a hotel in mind so we already had a lot of the facilities that a conference hotel would want, like conference rooms at hotel standard. That was one of the advantages of building a stadium to a high standard because the existing conference rooms and facilities were all built to 4-star hotel standards. So all we really needed to add on to give ourselves a 4-star hotel were a restaurant, bars, reception facilities, a gym and of course bedrooms.

'Then we had to go and convince the bank. We got separate funding that was ring-fenced for running the hotel. We formed a separate company, a 50–50 joint venture with the De Vere Group.'

Obviously the joint venture with De Vere took months of planning, and it would be years before it would start making a positive contribution to club funds. But in the summer of 1998 Wanderers also needed a short-term fix to prevent the bank from losing patience. It was at this point in time that Eddie Davies – successful businessman and long-time friend of Gartside – entered the equation.

'I had known Eddie for about 10 years and knew he was interested in the club,' says Gartside. 'Even so I wasn't very comfortable with calling him and asking him to help out, but we were absolutely desperate. I told him about the situation and said that if he wanted to do something it would be fantastic, but if he didn't I would fully understand. The bank had said we needed to find a minimum amount of equity which was around £2million. We had put feelers out to anybody who was interested and we received help from a variety of sources and then got money in from the rest of the directors. Then Eddie came up trumps with a cheque that sorted out the problem in the short term.'

All this manoeuvring was carried out away from prying eyes, but the outside world got an inkling of the extent of the financial pressures when the club failed to renew the contract of former skipper Scott Sellers. Todd told the *Bolton Evening News* that he had identified several targets to bolster the squad

but, not surprisingly, when he went to the board he found the transfer cupboard was bare.

Despite the financial situation, Todd's focus was on trying to win promotion, and he desperately wanted to keep his side together. With the pressure mounting, what he needed more than anything was a good start to the new season – a start that suggested he could engineer another promotion tilt. A 2–1 win over Queen's Park Rangers in the opening game of the season at the Reebok with goals from Holdsworth and Gudjohnsen was promising. Sadly it then turned sour. A 1–0 defeat at home to Manchester City was sandwiched between losses at Ipswich and Charlton. Even a brilliant display from two-goal Per Frandsen against Birmingham City at the Reebok was only enough to earn a point – though the Dane did inspire a fight-back from 3–1 down to 3–3 that was worthy of better circumstances.

Seven games into the 1999–2000 season and Wanderers had a sorry six points. The club looked more like leaving the Division through the door marked 'Relegation' rather than the one marked 'Promotion'. To add to

The Hotel at the Reebok.

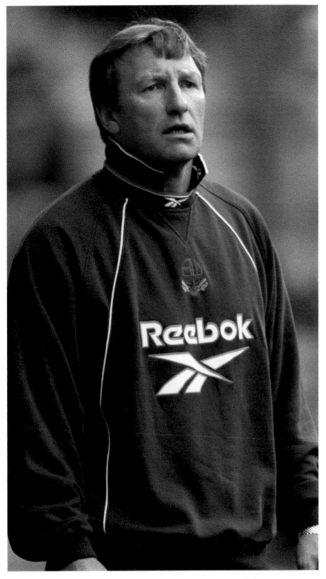

Anxious times: Colin Todd shortly before he stepped down as manager.

bid from Bradford for Frandsen (Todd valued him closer to 10 times that amount) but, following his heroics against Birmingham, the midfield star was once again attracting headlines over his future.

Finally, on 22 September 1999 Frandsen was sold to Blackburn Rovers for £1.75 million. By now the only surprise about the whole deal was the relatively small fee the club had felt forced to accept. Then shock news from the Reebok came the same day and completely overshadowed the loss of the influential midfield man. Todd felt he couldn't live with the sale of Frandsen and tendered his own resignation. For him it was a clear indication of future club policy, and he didn't want any part of it.

the board's concerns, a crowd of just 11,668 showed up for the game against Birmingham. The club's cash worries were now common knowledge, with mounting newspaper speculation about the impending sale of stars like Fish and Frandsen. In the summer Wanderers had rejected a cheeky £1 million

'The board were changing and they wanted to take a different tack,' he said. 'When the club decided to sell Per it was the final straw as far as I was concerned, and so I decided to resign. I had sensed the danger for some time. Even so, resigning was a very sad day for me, but the pressure had been mounting, not so much from the supporters, although we hadn't started the season well, but from inside the club. Whether the decision to sell Per was right or wrong, well – I think the fact that the club brought him back a few months later answers that one. Despite what happened I will always look back on my time at Bolton as hugely enjoyable. There were some great highs and a few lows, but I'm proud of the job I did there and the quality of players I brought to the club.'

Although the event had been preceded by weeks of speculation, the speed of the sale surprised the man at the centre of it. Says Frandsen, 'It came right out of the blue. I remember going into training one day and being told that the club had received an offer for me, and they asked me to speak to Blackburn Rovers. It all went through very quickly. When I look back, I suppose I should never have gone. My heart was still at Bolton, and I wasn't really happy at Blackburn. I guess I was sold to help balance the books, but I don't know, you would have to ask somebody else about that.'

The upheaval at the Reebok didn't end at losing the star player and manager. A few weeks later it was announced that the man who had helped make the Reebok vision become a reality, chairman Gordon Hargreaves, had stepped down too. As the sale of Frandsen had dramatically demonstrated, Gartside's pragmatic approach had won the internal power struggle. Publicly the new chairman heaped praise on his predecessor, telling the *Bolton Evening News* 'The club has moved forward faster during his period as chairman than at any other time in its history. Relocation was a big decision, and Gordon handled it superbly. He deserves the chance now to step down and enjoy his football.'

At the time Gartside tried to pour cold water on any talk of a board-level rift, but in actual fact he says he had taken control of the club several weeks previously and had sanctioned the sale of Frandsen.

'It was made pretty clear around the time Eddie got involved that we had to make wholesale changes and some of the board members weren't willing to make those changes – they still felt that they wanted to run it the same way,' he says. 'It was obvious to me that we had to do something, and it was time to put up or shut up. In effect I took

Fans' fury: supporters showed their feelings at the Reebok.

over as chairman in the August, although it was only confirmed in October, but I started from the August at the beginning of the season.

'It was a difficult time because it was a case of having to be pretty ruthless with people that I had enjoyed a friendship with for more than 10 years. I had to take some pretty hard decisions about people and about how we were going to run the club, but I had to be firm because otherwise it wouldn't work. So in time Gordon Hargreaves, Graham Ball and Brian Scowcroft all left the board.'

Having assumed command, Gartside was faced with his first major public test as Wanderers chairman – finding Todd's

successor. In the meantime it was left to the departed boss's long-time chief coach Phil Brown to look after the playing staff while the search was conducted. If the board had hoped Brown would keep the hot seat warm in silence, they were going to be disappointed. For Brown, a former captain, was desperate for the chance to manage the team. He knew his lack of front-line experience would count against him and that the best way to press his case was going to be over the following few weeks when he had a chance to show what he could do.

'As far as I was concerned it was my big opportunity because I really wanted the job,' he says.

Brown's first chance to impress came at the Reebok against Nottingham Forest. The match was also Wanderers' supporters' first chance to voice their feelings about the recent departures of Frandsen and Todd. The game was played out to a continuous background chorus of 'Sack the Board'. However, the mood was lifted when defender Neil Cox grabbed an injury-time winner in a thrilling 3–2 triumph as Wanderers came back from 2–1 down. It wasn't just the victory, it was the manner of the performance that left seasoned watchers in little doubt that Brown had won over the Reebok dressing room – though he still had to convince the men in the boardroom

Gudni Bergsson, by then an elder statesman in the dressing room, came out publicly in support of the caretaker's bid. 'When the news broke that Per was going to Blackburn it took a lot of the players by surprise. Per had been a key man for us, and we were surprised that he was going to go, but we knew the decision was down to financial reasons. As a group, players tend to sense that there are financial pressures and that things aren't quite right, but it's not something we tend to dwell on. But, of

course, we realised that there was pressure on the club, we weren't daft and we could read the papers. I think we all realised that there wasn't too much money at the club and that was underlined when Per was sold.

'But what could we do? We had our contracts and we were professionals who were still being paid. That's pretty much how you get on with things when there are major changes at a club. You just knuckle down. We had to because we had games to play; we had to get on with it. Phil Brown did a great job at that time and there was some speculation about Phil getting the job on a permanent basis. I think it would have been a decision that the players wouldn't have objected to, because there would have been the element of continuity.'

Brown's credentials were further enhanced a week after the Forest match when the caretaker inspired a newly-galvanised Wanderers to a 4–0 win away at Swindon. Defeat next time out at Wolves proved to be a temporary blip. Brown made up for that set-back by leading Wanderers to a League Cup win away at Premier League Derby County. He made it four wins out of five when Ricardo Gardner scored the only goal against Huddersfield at the Reebok.

'I had been surprised at the start we'd made that season,' says Brown. 'I'd gone into it fully expecting us to do a lot better than we did. But when Colin left we were in a really precarious position. We were on the edge of the kind of precipice that Nottingham Forest and Sheffield Wednesday later went over. The results I achieved when I was caretaker really strengthened my hand. I wanted the job, but with hindsight I went about it in the wrong way. My mistake was that I put a lot of pressure on the board and the chairman. I made a lot of public pronouncements in the press when all they really did was make his decision more difficult. I think I learnt that it's not good to back your chairman into a corner.'

While results were doing at least some of Brown's talking for him, Gartside and his fellow directors were looking at other alternatives. Bruce Rioch, whose success with Bolton in the early 1990s had landed him the Arsenal manager's job, was back in the frame, as was former Liverpool boss Roy Evans.

'One of the people I have always attributed a lot of the current success to is Bruce Rioch,' says Gartside. 'Before he arrived there was

almost an acceptance at the club that we weren't ever going to be successful again. But he came and forced us into making certain decisions when they needed to be made. It is a pity in some respects that Bruce didn't stay because I think he probably deserved some of the benefits of what we did, but it was his choice to leave.

'After Colin had resigned we went to see Bruce, and we could have had him back but he had a relationship with the previous chairman who was still on the board at that stage. As much as it might have been a reasonable football decision, I think it would have been an unhealthy way to manage the club. We also interviewed Roy Evans, who had been at Liverpool. But all Roy talked about were the type of players who were earning £15,000 a week. At the time we couldn't afford £15,000-a-week players so that counted against him.'

Then there was Sam Allardyce. In the early 1970s Dudley-born Allardyce arrived at Bolton as a 15-year-old. He stayed for the best part of a decade, forging a Good Cop, Bad Cop defensive partnership with Paul Jones. Allardyce played the tough enforcer to Jones's cultured footballer. A powerful header of the ball, he also had a habit of scoring spectacular and often vital goals. Even after moves to Sunderland, Millwall, Tampa Bay, Huddersfield, Coventry and Preston North End, Big Sam's heart was always in Bolton. He'd married a Bolton girl, returned to the club for a second spell in the mid 1980s and actually applied for the manager's job around the time when Charlie Wright was axed.

After hanging up his boots, Allardyce was given a couple of assistant manager assignments before being given his first break as a manager of Limerick in Ireland, before impressive stints with Blackpool and Notts County in the lower Leagues.

'If you took the name Sam Allardyce off the top and looked at his CV, it had everything,' says Gartside. 'I didn't know Sam as a person – yes, he had been one of my heroes as a footballer – but until we interviewed him I'd never spoken to him. So, unlike some of the others on the board, I had no feelings one way or another about him. In that respect it was a clean interview. Sam's CV impressed me because he'd had to scrap. He'd been at Limerick where he had to go collecting with the local priest on a Friday night. They would go in pubs and try to get money into the hat to pay the players' wages on a Saturday. We weren't quite at that level,

Arrival: Sam Allardyce strikes the customary pose for the photographers after being unveiled as Bolton boss in October 1999.

but the principle was good. He understood that you needed money. He'd been a coach, an academy coach, an assistant manager and a manager. And he had been at clubs in difficult circumstances.

'Of course, I didn't know how successful he would be, and I am not going to claim that I had a vision the day we interviewed him that we were going to be where we are now, but I did know that the guy had the attributes to actually work with us. It was going to have to be one of those jobs where you had to work together. Coming to the club when he did it was never going to be an easy job, for us or for him, and there was always going to be conflict – there's always conflict in football.

'In my book the most important relationship in a football club is the one between the chairman and the manager. It's got to be one of total trust. You can't have it any other way. I have recognised that through 18-plus years of being involved in football at boardroom level. I can tell when a club is going to have a problem because their manager and their chairman have got issues. For me the whole structure of a club is not right when the chairman and manager don't get on and that runs through onto the football pitch.'

Despite's Phil Brown's purple patch as caretaker, Allardyce was appointed manager of Bolton Wanderers on his 45th birthday, 19 October 1999. He was presented to the Reebok crowd that night when Crewe were the visitors. Though Allardyce took the plaudits, Brown selected the side. Unfortunately Crewe decided to spoil the party, and the Big Sam era got off to a stuttering start with a 2–2 draw.

'Because of the way things had gone, I was absolutely gutted when Sam was announced as manager,' says Brown. 'He knows that, because we've spoken about it, and I would never have held a grudge if he had decided to get rid of me there and then. I know that there were people advising him that he should let me go because of certain things I'd said when I was caretaker. When we sat down together for the first time he asked me if I'd carry on being first-team coach. But I told him I wanted the assistant manager's job, and I also pledged never to undermine his position by chasing every job that came along, and I think we developed a mutual respect. He had my word and we went on to work well together.'

In fact, it wasn't the first time the pair had worked together. 'I'd been with Sam at

Blackpool as a player, and I knew then that he was destined for great things. I could see that he had something about him. I really wanted to work with him while I was at Blackpool.'

So much so that Brown took a big pay cut to move from being a player to being the first-team coach at Blackpool. 'It was a big risk for me and my family, but I think Sam always respected me for it. There were a few of us from the Blackpool days. We'd taken Blackpool to the Play-offs, but when Sam got sacked we'd all gone our separate ways. But before long Mark Taylor, the physio, and Jack Chapman, the scout, who'd all worked together there got back together at Bolton.

'It was like getting the band back together, and we all shared the various experiences that we'd been through in the intervening years and brought them to the table. By that stage Sam and I were closing on a UEFA Pro-Licence coaching level, and Mark Taylor had advanced as a physio, and Jack, well, there was no one with more experience than Jack in the scouting game.'

On being offered the job, Allardyce had been made fully aware of the club's perilous financial position, and despite the money from the Frandsen deal the new man was expected to wheel and deal the club out of trouble.

'The only ambition at that point was to survive financially,' he says. 'So the trick I had to try to pull off was to help make sure the bank were happy by resolving the financial problems in the short term and still push things forward on the football side. It was the usual experience of life in the lower divisions. You learn to live with short-term fixes. It's what we'd done at Blackpool and Notts County. You borrow players off other people to get by and to try to be successful. But I felt that if you were prepared to sell your players off at 'fire sale' prices then you were never going to really resolve the financial problems in the long term. I was only going to help the club in the short term by trying to resist attempts to sell players at low valuations. That was the biggest problem that I had at first because the club wanted to sell players and I didn't want to.'

In the end a compromise was reached. Allardyce moved on the fringe members of his squad and managed to keep hold of his stars – for the time being at least.

'We knew that by doing that we would be doing less harm to the team. Then we brought in loan players to compensate for the loss of the players who had gone. And a lot of those new players were better than the ones we got rid of.'

The first signings arrived in December: John O`Kane and Gareth Farrelly – the man whose goal for the Toffees two years earlier had effectively condemned Bolton to relegation. They both arrived on loan with a view to long-term deals, a policy which was to become an Allardyce transfer trademark.

However, the money – or rather the lack of it – wasn't the new manager's only concern.

'When I came here on day one it was like walking into a brand new stadium with a rusty boot in the cupboard,' he said, 'There was an antiquated mentality. The club still had the burden of the Burnden Park administration in terms of the structure and the way the football club was being run.

'It was a club that lived in the past and never looked to the future. One of the first tasks I had was to bring the day-to-day running and management up to the same level as the stadium. Certainly that was the aspiration. I had to make a shift in the mentality. There were lots of people that I

had known when I played at Burnden as a kid, and although it was right to still have them around, a lot still had the same mentality. I knew that Bolton Wanderers would never be successful unless that mentality changed.'

Allardyce says that while people within the club may have remembered him as the big centre-half, they didn't know much about the journey he had been on since.

Sam Allardyce the manager was determined to introduce a whole new way of thinking to the club – even if that meant saying goodbye to long-standing members of the club's staff.

'I felt that the only way forward was to create a forward thinking mentality that was creative, proactive rather than reactive and visionary. It wasn't in place at that particular time. I had to strip the club down and get rid of the past to help create it. Nobody likes change so I had to be ruthless.'

Allardyce's modernisation plans weren't greeted with universal approval. 'The directors and the chairman all had to be persuaded that it was the right thing to do because there were many relationships and friendships built up over several years, but those friendships and relationships were not necessarily going to enhance the club.'

Big Sam's other plan was a little easier to stomach – winning football matches. And the degree of success that season was absolutely staggering considering he was at the helm of a club in crisis.

His first game in charge ended in a 2–1 defeat at Norwich which was followed up by a 1–1 draw at Nottingham Forest. Allardyce notched up his first win at the Reebok on 30 October, though his team made him wait for it. It wasn't until the 87th minute

On target: Eidur Gudjohnsen celebrates after scoring in the League Cup against Wimbledon.

when Bob Taylor opened the scoring against Swindon then Bo Hansen grabbed a second goal. That sparked a welcome winning sequence in the League, while in the Carling Cup Eidur Gudjohnsen scored a fantastic solo effort in the quarter-final against Wimbledon at the Reebok to set up a 2–1 win. Lo and behold the semi-finals beckoned.

The first leg at the Reebok against Tranmere ended in a 1–0 defeat, after a rather lifeless performance. The second leg, a 3–0 hammering at Prenton Park, left Allardyce fuming and having to issue a public apology to the fans. Despite that set-back and an initially difficult period of adjustment to the new boss, Bergsson says it didn't take long for the players to warm to their new manager.

'I had met him a few times, and I knew all about his links with the club, so I was quite excited by his arrival, and when we learned

Exit: Big Sam can hardly watch as Bolton lose to Tranmere in the League Cup semi-final.

that Phil was to stay on as his number two that was good. Sam was a larger-than-life character, and it was difficult not to be smitten by his infectious enthusiasm on the pitch and off it.

'From a football perspective it took us a few weeks to get used to one another and to know what he wanted us to do. Colin Todd's focus was on the team's possession of the ball. He was very clear that that was what he wanted, whereas Big Sam wanted us to get the ball down and play with pace and power. Colin was a great defender in his time and, like Sam, was keen on keeping a clean sheet, but that wasn't his main focus, whereas Sam was always emphasising the importance of keeping it tight and being difficult to break down. It was difficult certainly at the

beginning to get used to what Sam wanted us to do but, in a nutshell, I think he made us a more difficult side to beat.

'After two or three months the side were on a good run and the last few weeks of the season we were really flying. It turned out to be a very memorable season.'

Indeed Wanderers made up for their defeat in the Worthington Cup semi-final by going on a memorable FA Cup run. They saw off Cardiff, Grimsby and Cambridge to set up a quarter-final tie against Division One leaders Charlton at the Reebok.

Eidur Gudjohnsen turned in another brilliant display and capped it with the only goal of the game. Wanderers, the first Wembley FA Cup winners back in 1923, were returning to the Twin Towers for a semi-final against Aston Villa – for a place in the last Final before the stadium was to close for redevelopment. How sweet it would be if the club could make a return trip.

In the event the Villa semi-final match will always be remembered by Bolton fans for Dean Holdsworth's miss in the dying minutes of normal time after a great cut back from Gudjohnsen. The striker had earlier struck a post with a free-kick as Bolton's luck failed to

Cup run: Ricardo Gardner pictured during Bolton's FA Cup third-round win over Cardiff at the Reebok in December.

Wembley way: FA Cup semi-final day, and Bolton and Aston Villa fans mix on Wembley Way.

Spot of pain: Bolton players hold their heads in their hands as they lose the FA Cup semi-final against Aston Villa at Wembley in a penalty shoot-out.

Hair-raiser: disappointed Wanderers fans following the penalty shoot-out defeat against Aston Villa.

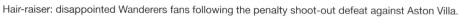

match their outstanding overall play. The match finished 0–0 after extra-time, and Villa won the penalty shoot-out 4–1.

'I suppose the Villa game at Wembley stands out for me,' says Holdsworth. 'It was a fantastic day and a disappointing day. To be able to play at Wembley was superb, and the atmosphere was brilliant. But to lose on penalties was terrible. I remember I scored my penalty, but it just wasn't to be our day.'

Despite their indifferent start, Wanderers had climbed up the League, but having already suffered two semi-final heartbreaks their hopes were now pinned on reaching the Play-offs for the second successive season. Their slow start to the season and the transition to the new manager's style had meant Wanderers were playing catch-up.

As the season reached the business end, Bolton renewed their fierce rivalry with Wolves who, along with Birmingham and Huddersfield, were contesting the last two Play-off places.

The two Wanderers faced one another in the penultimate game of the season in a Reebok thriller. Wolves took the lead, thanks to Ludovic Pollet, in first-half injury time, but goals from Claus Jensen and Eidur

Gudjohnsen helped secure a third successive win for Allardyce's side. It was their eighth in 12 games, and the three points meant that going into the final game of the season, at home to Norwich, Wanderers were just a point behind sixth-placed Huddersfield. Wolves, following their Reebok defeat, were two points adrift of Bolton and three behind Huddersfield.

The Yorkshire side faced a difficult test with a trip to champions Fulham on the final day.

'After the Aston Villa defeat at Wembley we said we wanted to be in it right to the end of the season,' Gudjohnsen told the *Bolton Evening News*. 'And that's what we managed to do. We did everything we could to keep the pressure on the other teams.'

Against Norwich, Holdsworth atoned for his Villa miss and scored the only goal to clinch Wanderers' place in the Play-offs. Huddersfield went down to a 3–0 defeat at Craven Cottage and Wolves managed a win, but their victory was in vain.

For the second successive season Bolton faced Ipswich Town in the Play-offs. And for the second year in succession the tie was to prove a dramatic one. This time it was

Talking tactics: Bolton boss Sam Allardyce prepares the side for extra-time in the Play-off match at Ipswich.

Wanderers who were left nursing broken hearts.

After just 26 minutes of the first leg Wanderers had taken a two-goal lead at the Reebok thanks to Holdsworth and Gudjohnsen. But Ipswich hit back and the game finished 2–2.

The second leg at Portman Road on 18 May 2000 was pulsating. It finished Ipswich 5 Wanderers 3. But that doesn't tell the half of it. Bolton ended the night with just nine men after a refereeing display from Orpington official Barry Knight that left Wanderers apoplectic with rage.

Gordon Sharrock, in the *Bolton Evening News,* summed up Knight's performance thus: 'Some

of his decisions were correct, others were staggeringly wrong. Even that wily old campaigner Tony Mowbray, the Ipswich player-coach, described his handling of the game as 'bizarre'. And the fact that it came in one of the most important games in the recent history of Bolton Wanderers – a game on which the club's future welfare depended – makes it all the more galling.'

Knight-mare: referee Barry Knight shows the red card to Bolton's Robbie Elliott as the side's Play-off hopes disappear.

For Bergsson the events were particularly infuriating because it could well have spelled the end of his career.

'The Play-off game at Ipswich was an incredible game and one I will never forget for all sorts of reasons,' says Bergsson. 'We prepared for it well, but on the night it was the refereeing display which we felt aggrieved about. Leading up to the game there was a lot of speculation about whether this would be my last season.

'My contract was up, I hadn't made a decision on my future, and it could have been that that was my last ever game in a Bolton shirt.

'Leaving the field I was thinking 'That can't be my last game''.

Looking back Allardyce still fumes at Knight's handling of the match: 'We were three minutes away from going through until he gave the worst refereeing display ever in the history of refereeing! That said, I still feel we blew it at the Reebok when we were 2–0 up.

'That Play-off defeat really made life extremely difficult for all of us because I knew then that the club's major assets were about to be stripped!'

One Season wonders

1. Fernando Hierro
2. Fredi Bobic
3. Bernard Mendy
4. Stig Tofting
5. Paul Ritchie
6. Matt Clarke
7. Allan Johnston
8. Hidetoshi Nakata
9. Vincent Candela
10. Jon Newsome

1999–2000

Ins

Gareth Farrelly (Everton), Franck Passi (SD Compostela), Allan Johnston (loan, Sunderland), Kevin Nolan (Trainee), David Norris (Boston United), Paul Ritchie (loan, Hearts).

Outs

Neil Cox (Watford), Andy Todd (Charlton Athletic), Mark Fish (Charlton Athletic), Paul Ritchie (Hearts), Scott Sellars (Huddersfield Town), Bob Taylor (West Bromwich Albion), Allan Johnston (loan, Sunderland).

Chapter Four

Going Up, Definitely Maybe

Summer 2000 and for the second time in 12 months Bolton Wanderers had to come to terms with a Play-off defeat.

The immediate fall-out of the Knight-mare at Ipswich was the departure from the Reebok of two of the club's major playing assets. Neither was a surprise. Claus Jensen went to newly-promoted Charlton for £4 million and striker Eidur Gudjohnsen went to Chelsea for a similar fee. With popular winger Michael Johansen also deciding to return to his native Denmark after his Bolton contract expired, the team that Todd had built and Allardyce honed was breaking up.

South African defender Mark Fish, a cult hero since his £2.5 million move from Lazio in August 1997, almost went with them. He only remained because a proposed £1.5 million move to Charlton fell through on medical grounds.

Departures: Michael Johansen and Eidur Gudjohnsen, who both moved on from the Reebok in the summer of 2000.

The price of the club's Play-off defeat was there for all to see. Yet this time around the sales of big-name playing assets didn't elicit the same response from the man in the Reebok hot seat. Disappointment yes, but Allardyce knew all about the reality of the financial situation when he arrived at the club the previous October. Indeed, but for the runs in the FA Cup and League Cup, both Gudjohnsen and Jensen would probably have been sold far sooner. Not that the departures of such talented players made the task of regaining the club's Premier League status any easier. The only silver lining this time was the size of the fees.

'When I first came in, players like Eidur Gudjohnsen and Claus Jensen would've been sold for £1.5 or £2 million, whereas what we'd managed to do by reaching two semi-finals and the Play-offs was to increase their value,' says Allardyce. 'Even at £4 million I reckon Eidur was undervalued, but he had to go because we needed the money, and we needed it quick. The other thing we managed to do that first season was bring in more revenue than expected by being successful in the Carling Cup, in the FA Cup and in the League, by getting into the Play-offs.'

Gartside acknowledges that Allardyce played a key role in maximising the value of the players who left the club around that period: 'Earlier that year we were at a point where we had to sell. We could have sold either Claus or Eidur before the end of the 1999–2000 season, but Sam was highly influential in convincing me that we had to hold onto them. We managed to support him on that, but he knew that at the end of that season if we didn't get promotion we would have to offload a couple of players. Their sales would at least generate some funds for him to be able to put some back into the club.'

Despite the headline departures the financial picture was changing, albeit slowly, as Gartside and Duckworth's new business plan started to take shape – quite literally in the case of the De Vere Whites Hotel, which was being constructed inside the South Stand.

It had been a controversial project from the off because, on the surface at least, it appeared as though the club was taking its eye off the ball. Supporters were asking how the club could afford to build a hotel at a time when they were selling their best players. They weren't the only ones.

'When we first proposed the idea 12 months earlier we had to go to shareholders for approval,' explains Duckworth. 'I remember being in that shareholders' meeting and saying that we had to take a long-term view. I knew I had to convince them that it was a good idea and that in years to come the hotel was going to actually be a benefit to the football club by bringing money back in. In the Reebok we had a stadium that was going to cost us a lot of money anyway just to run. The other thing I had to explain was that the funding for the hotel was completely separate from the football side.'

Duckworth told the meeting that the £10 million was only being lent in order to build the hotel – it would not have been loaned to spend on players. 'The bank was only backing the plan because they knew we were putting the money into a separate company, away from the football side of things, in order to build an asset that would then earn money.'

The hotel deal was significant in other ways too, because it helped to convince people that the club was serious about trying to build a firm base for the future, people like Eddie Davies. Says Duckworth, 'In my view I

don't think there is a cat-in-hell's chance that Eddie would have put money in if he thought that the club was going to be run in any other way than as a business. That is an essential part of his philosophy. He believes that whatever the organisation, a football club or whatever, you run it as a business. It was very much a condition of his in 1999 that if he was going to put money into the club then he had to look at the numbers to start with and agree our strategy. He didn't get involved day to day, but he was kept very much informed and attended regular board meetings.'

Just as the hotel project progressed nicely, another sign of positive progress came on 15 and 16 July when the stadium opened the turnstiles to a new kind of supporter. Crowds of 30,000-plus on both days turned out to see Mancunian rock giants Oasis in concert. It was enough to get them dancing in the boardroom – for here were Wanderers at last taking advantage of the Reebok to generate cash from non-football activities.

All of which was very encouraging; however, the sales of Gudjohnsen and Jensen merely helped to service the long-term debt. They did very little to help a manager planning a promotion campaign. Allardyce,

Rock and roll stars: a packed Reebok plays host to rock giants Oasis.

who had a burning ambition to manage in the Premier League, was still expected to wheel and deal in the transfer market in the hope of unearthing bargains. Amid the transfer gloom, there was one piece of good news when Allardyce was allowed to spend £1.2 million to bring Per Frandsen back to the club less than 12 months after his move to Blackburn Rovers.

'Everything was about not spending any money or, if you really had to, spending as little money as you possibly could,' says Allardyce. 'We had to overcome that by finding other ways of getting what we wanted. For instance, sports psychologist Mike Forde initially came here on a basis of 'If you're successful you get paid, if you're not, you won't get anything'. Of course, it is very difficult to get somebody here of his quality on that kind of arrangement. But we managed to persuade his company to work like that by saying that if you're successful with us you can use our name to promote your company. Fortunately they agreed. That was typical of many of the deals we negotiated. We even did it for our supplies of bottled water!'

The good news defensively was that Allardyce had at least managed to persuade lynchpin Gudni Bergsson not to retire following the Ipswich Play-off defeat.

Bergsson recalls 'It was the end of my contract, and I was approaching my 35th birthday, and I was wondering whether that Ipswich game would be my last game. But it had been a memorable season for the team, and I was enjoying my football so I decided I would play one more season. Sam had certainly given me my appetite back so, although my family decided to move back to Iceland – we had planned it that way so that my children could go to school there – my wife and I decided that I would give it one more season, and so that's what I did.

'The way the Ipswich game had ended was a real sickener for us. We felt aggrieved, and I felt grateful that Sam was able to give me a chance to carry on for one more year. Even despite the loss of Eidur and Claus, we still had a good set of players and a good mix of experience and desire in the squad, and now Sam was able to put his mark on the team. We were really determined to go one better than we had in the previous two seasons. Right from the start there was nothing else in the squad but a determination to go up.'

Allardyce says he didn't have to work too hard to convince his skipper to stick with the side.

'Gudni had been thinking about retiring, but it wasn't hard to talk him around. The biggest problem was with his family going back to Iceland. But Gudni needed to play as long as he could, and because of our success the season before it made his decision easy. I think that if we hadn't been successful he would have packed in. From my point of view, if he'd gone back to Iceland then he'd have soon regretted it.'

It was a vital decision as, despite his age, Bergsson remained a vital member of Allardyce's squad.

'For me he was key. He was the core of the team. A top, top player. I remember saying to him I wish I'd had him as a 25-year-old. As far as I am concerned Gudni should have played in the Premier League all his career. He could easily have played for a much bigger club than Bolton. He should've played for one of the top four clubs because he had everything you need in his game. He had pace, he had ability on the ball, he was a good header and he read the game well. If you're looking for negatives, I'd say he maybe wasn't

Leaders: influential Gudni Bergsson has a word with teammate Per Frandsen.

the best of talkers, but that was probably because the game was so easy for him. That said, I don't think people had ever actually taught him the art of defending in its entirety until he came here. He knew about what it meant to be working in a unit and to defend the unit, which helped him a great deal. I can't believe a big club let him go when he had so much ability. He could've played for Liverpool, or Man United, whoever he wanted to.'

If Bergsson the player impressed Allardyce, the Bolton boss was equally as struck by Bergsson the man.

'We used to share long conversations, for many hours. We had a good relationship, and I thoroughly enjoyed my time with him. Gudni was an intelligent guy, not just in football terms, but in how he thought about life in general.'

That relationship was important. For it meant that Allardyce had a key ally in the dressing room at a time when he was trying to bring about a mini revolution in the way the club looked after its players. Inspired by what he had discovered as a player in 1983 when he joined the NASL side Tampa Bay Rowdies, Allardyce was determined to introduce the levels of scientific thinking that were regarded as normal for professional sports organisations in the United States some 20 years earlier.

'At Tampa the soccer team had close connections with the local American Football outfit the Tampa Bay Buccaneers,' recalls Big Sam. 'I was fascinated by how they looked after their professional athletes, and being typically American they were happy to throw open the door to me and let me speak to them. They were just so organised and professional. They had something like 60 players on their roster, and the way they were looked after was incredible. They had everything covered. They looked at things we in football back then had never really considered: things like the nutritional values of the food they ate and the juices they drank. They looked at the benefits of rehydration. Then there was the medical side. That was huge. They had all sorts of people and huge, expensive scanning equipment. They had developed a number of special strappings for muscles. On the playing side they had a coach for each position. These days football has followed suit, but back then it was a totally new concept. They also employed sports psychologists. At the time I have to admit that I thought that psychologists were for weak people, but gradually over time I started to understand the benefits they could bring to a team and to an individual.'

It was a world away from the slice of orange at half-time and cold water on a 'magic' sponge for injuries. No wonder Allardyce was in awe. That period of his playing career was short, but it was to have a major bearing on his thinking, and he started to introduce some of the elements to the Reebok. Though not without a degree of resistance.

'We brought in a lot of changes almost from day one,' says Allardyce. 'Initially the players moaned at everything we did because players are like that; they hate change. We took their tea away in the dressing room, they moaned. We changed the pre-match meal, they moaned. We changed the training times, they moaned. We started to do ice baths, they moaned!'

In assistant Phil Brown Allardyce had a strong advocate in favour of introducing new concepts to improve the playing squad's performance levels – even if the advances weren't immediately embraced by the players

themselves. It was Brown, in fact, who had initially introduced psychologist Mike Forde to the club during his successful spell as caretaker.

'When we brought Mike in he was given a really hard time by the players, but we knew sports psychology was an important side of the game,' says Brown.

'You often heard people talk about being mentally tough or saying that 90 percent of games are won and lost in the dressing room – and yet so little was done about looking at ways to improve the mentality of players. I felt very strongly that we had to do something. We now have coaches for goalkeepers, for defenders; there are specialist coaches here, there and everywhere, but even now few people in the game seem to look at the mental side and develop an approach on how to improve that.

'Mike was battered by the players verbally when he first came in, but he stuck at it and saw things through. We realised that we were on a journey of discovery and that success was the end goal for all the staff, including Mike.'

Other changes were just as radical. Allardyce was a swift and vocal convert to the

The Reebok Stadium, home of Bolton Wanderers.

ProZone system, which uses several cameras around the pitch, which are linked to sophisticated computer software. It tracks the exact movements of each and every player on the pitch at any one time. ProZone allowed the manager and his coaching staff to assess their players and opposition players with incredibly accurate data. The tough part for the manager was convincing the right people that the investment in ProZone and the like was needed.

'Sometimes the directors had difficulties because they couldn't understand what we were doing. It's difficult to explain to somebody that spending money now is going to be beneficial later on, especially when they've never done it before. Don't get me wrong, they knew about football and they loved their football, but they didn't always understand what I felt was needed to get us to where we wanted to go.

'The chairman had no choice with me. I had to mither him to get my way and find a way of doing it in the end. Sometimes it was easier than others. Sometimes he would say yes straight away. But most of the time it came down to funds. I always laid out how we were going to afford it. It was a case of

finding a way to do it. The chairman and I were constantly falling out, but you always fall out in business. You can't work with a chairman in a football club and be nice to him all the time. What happens is you fall out and then the next day you resolve your differences and move on. Of course, you want to have a friendship with the guy, but that friendship can't get in the way of doing business. It can't get in the way of disagreeing with each other for one reason or another.

'You need to have a relationship where you are able to say what you think. That way you will disagree from time to time but then you come to a solution. Sometimes you win, sometimes you don't, but, whatever, you've got to be able to get on with things and move on.

'But persuading them to get ProZone in was a massive financial commitment at that particular time. We were one of the very first clubs outside of the Premier League to have ProZone, but the learning tool was absolutely crucial to our development. In the end we did a deal with ProZone in which we agreed to openly promote it.

'We would get the TV cameras into the club and use all our sales skills as well as our football skills to promote it. The fact that we didn't have to pass any cash over to get what we wanted was great for the club, but this kind of arrangement only really works if you're successful on the field.

'It all adds a little bit more to the pressure of being a manager. The sales pitch to the directors back then was that the cheapest way to be successful was to have the biggest back room staff, because the size of the back room staff's wages compared to the size of one player's wages was tiny. Over the years the backroom staff grew from just four to around 18 and the part timers became full timers. The sports science team grew from one part timer to three full timers. Physios went from one, to two, to three. Then we got a player recruitment officer. Together these were huge key elements in helping us become successful.'

Phil Brown watched all this from close quarters. 'We were heavily in debt at that point, and so it was a constant battle for Sam to get what he wanted out of the board. They backed him if they could, but we desperately wanted to improve the training facilities and improve the team, and there were ideas that he wanted to implement.

'When Sam had come back to Bolton there were still a lot of misconceptions about him because of the way he had played the game. He was a big, brash centre-half. Sometimes he would play along with that image if he could gain from it, but he hasn't actually succeeded as a manager because of his physical power. He has succeeded because of his drive and determination and his other skills.'

Despite Allardyce's protestations, his chairman shared many of his frustrations. 'It was a nightmare,' says Gartside. 'On the one hand we were trying to balance the books, and at the same time we were conscious of trying to give Sam money to spend and give him the right facilities.

'The Reebok was a great stadium, but as a club it was as though we had the Rolls-Royce on the drive but we couldn't afford the petrol. But I simply could not go to Sam and say here's a blank sheet of paper, tell me what you want, because we didn't have the money to do that. It was more a case of saying to him "OK, let's identify some opportunities that will help take us to the next level then we'll see whether we can find you the money." It was a strategy born out of necessity because we couldn't afford to go and speculate. When we started to have some success the challenge was trying to keep pace with that success.'

Money may well have been in short supply, but team spirit certainly wasn't. Having come close for two successive seasons, the squad, galvanised by the returning Frandsen, entered the 2000–01 season determined to make up for their two previous Play-off disappointments.

Says Dean Holdsworth, 'Despite some of the big name departures, I think we had a point to prove – there was almost an anger among the players. The desire was there for all to see. At the start of the season we sat down and between us we set a target of 92 points – two points per game.'

It may have sounded ambitious and, after the Reebok curtain raiser finished in a 1–1 draw against Burnley, it looked it. But Wanderers then reeled off an impressive six successive wins to put themselves up among the early leaders – Fulham, Watford and Blackburn Rovers.

'I think it was the heartbreak from the season before that had really given us an appetite, a desire to do something,' says Holdsworth. 'You could smell the hunger, the anger that had built up over a couple of

seasons. The players all knew their jobs, and we had squad players who could come in and do a job. There was also a fantastic atmosphere building up around the club. We would go paint balling or out to the races together. We genuinely enjoyed each other's company on and off the field, and I liked that. We also had a nucleus of players who knew how to win matches, people like Paul Warhurst, Colin Hendry, Mike Whitlow and Per Frandsen, who had an absolutely superb season. We had a lot of belief in each other. During the season we held a lot of meetings as a team – these weren't the kind where you sit around drinking tea and eating bacon butties. These were meetings where all the players contributed. We all felt we could, and we all knew that the points we made would be taken on board – then everyone agreed that Sam was right in the first place!'

Under Allardyce, Holdsworth was a player transformed. Frustrated by his early form for the club, the striker had taken to the new manager almost straight away.

'When Sam took over he and the backroom staff worked to develop a five-year plan, and we all knew what the aims of the club were,' he says. 'I hadn't met Sam before

Head master: a revitalised Dean Holdsworth scores a hat-trick of headers against Scunthorpe in the FA Cup.

he became manager and wasn't too sure what to make of him at first, but he very quickly took me to one side and reassured me that he knew how to get the best out of me. I'd only scored one headed goal in the two years that I'd been at the club prior to his arrival, but that wasn't particularly my fault, it was the way we played the game. Sam was true to his word and brought in wingers Alan Johnson and Nicky Summerbee within a few weeks of being here and that helped me. I even scored a hat-trick of headers in an FA Cup game against Scunthorpe. I think that says a lot about Sam. It taught me that you've got to

play to your players' strengths, and Sam seemed to be fully aware of that and how to do it. But he was also big on team spirit. He put some trust and faith in me, for example he let me take the forwards for coaching, and that gave me a lift. I'd volunteer for extra training like several of the lads.'

Though Gudjohnsen had departed, Holdsworth soon found he had competition for a place up front from Michael Ricketts, who had been signed in the summer from Walsall for £250,000 – though even that relatively small deal nearly hit the buffers because of finance.

New faces: Michael Ricketts is mobbed by Gareth Farrelly after scoring his first Bolton goal.

'We actually struggled to find £250,000 to buy him in the first place because of the financial state we were in,' says Allardyce. Ricketts's burst of pace and deadly finishing made him the find of the season – and the fee helped establish the manager's credentials as one of the best bargain hunters in the business. Before arriving at Bolton, Ricketts had scored 15 goals in 90 appearances, hardly the kind of record that had suitors queuing up at the Bescot gates. But his impact at the Reebok was instant. Following in the footsteps of a crowd pleaser like Gudjohnsen was going to be a tall order for anyone, but it certainly didn't inhibit the burly Midlander. He was the find of the season.

Says Ricketts, 'In the previous season I had scored playing for Walsall at home when we beat Bolton 2–0 – we only had 10 men so I remember the game really well, and I guess Sam must have too. When I got to Bolton it was a little frustrating because I was suspended for the first couple of games that season. I made my debut in the third game when I came on against Preston and scored. I can still see it now. A ball was knocked through by Per Frandsen and I turned Michael Jackson on the halfway line and got

through and tucked it away, which was sweet. It is always nice to get a goal early in your career. It helps you settle down.'

Ricketts followed up his goals against Preston by coming off the bench to bag two at Huddersfield, then did the same to score the only goal of the game at Grimsby, and grabbed another off the bench against Portsmouth. By mid-September he had scored every time he had stepped off the bench – six in total – and naturally he picked up the tag super sub. But that was never going to last long. His performances were starting to demand a place in the starting line-up, and Allardyce knew it.

'I think I more or less slotted into the side straight way,' says Ricketts. 'We were playing 4–3–3 when we had the ball and 4–5–1 when we didn't and a lot of sides didn't know how to handle us. Sam found a formula that worked and has pretty much stuck to it since. Kevin Nolan and I were thick as thieves. He'd just broken into the side around that time too and was doing well, and we got on really well together. But then all my time at Bolton was pretty good.'

The striker's first start came at Ewood Park against a Blackburn Rovers side who, despite

I feel good: Holdsworth sparks Reebok celebrations with a goal against Wolves.

the death of their benefactor Jack Walker in August 2000, were shaping up to be strong promotion contenders under Graeme Souness. Ricketts failed to find the net, but Dane Bo Hansen grabbed a point with a goal two minutes from time.

Leaders Fulham, under manager Jean Tigana, were next up at the Reebok, and after being gifted a lead after just 15 seconds the Londoners went on to win comfortably 2–0. Still, seven wins from the first nine games was well ahead of Allardyce's schedule. What followed was a run that contained just one win in seven, when defensive frailties were exposed. Two late goals at Gillingham turned a 2–0 lead into a 2–2 draw, then in a bizarre game at Stockport Wanderers came back to square the match having been 3–0 down, only to lose it in injury time. October finished with Wanderers allowing Crystal Palace to snatch a point at the Reebok despite holding a 3–1 lead with only three minutes left on the clock!

Off the field, 30 October was a significant landmark for the club as it marked the official opening of the De Vere Whites Hotel. The 125-room four-star hotel suddenly gave the club earning capacity regardless of what happened on Saturday afternoons.

Over and out: defender Mark Fish departed under a cloud in November.

However, at that stage of the season Allardyce was hardly in a mood to celebrate. For early in November his defensive headaches got worse. Mark Fish and the club had failed to agree a contract extension, and with his current deal up at the end the season he would have been able to walk away in the summer as a free agent. Charlton, who had come close to agreeing a deal in June, were still interested in the defender and finally settled on a £700,000 bid for the player. The move wasn't without its controversy, as Allardyce had publicly slammed Fish's performance level in the weeks leading up to the transfer. However, in December the manager replaced Fish with experienced

Col-ossus: new signing Colin Hendry – scoring against Sheffield Wednesday – quickly made his mark at the club.

campaigner Colin Hendry on loan from Coventry City. Scotland international Hendry had a Premier League winners' medal from his time with Blackburn Rovers, and although 35 by the time he arrived at the Reebok he was wily enough to comfortably hold his own in Division One.

Hendry also found the move to the Reebok to his liking. For when he arrived he discovered a very progressive sports science and physio team using all the latest techniques and thinking to help extend his playing days. It was quite unlike anything he had come across in his career up to that point. While it may have been 21st-century thinking behind the scenes, Allardyce was patching up the playing squad with some good old-fashioned wheeler dealing.

'When you are a manager in the lower Leagues it is very much part of your job,' he says. 'You learn to manage and live with short-term fixes. You borrow players off other people to get by and to be successful.'

Allardyce made full use of the loan market – bringing players in on a temporary basis to fill positions as and when needed. If they did well he would try to find a way of engineering a permanent move. The Hendry situation was typical though by no means exceptional.

'The club's facilities looked great on the surface, but at the time we were just working from week to week and month to month,' says the manager. 'At the start of the season we'd brought in Isaiah Rankin, a forward

Bubbly boss: Sam Allardyce celebrates being named Manager of the Month for January.

from Bradford, and later that season got Colin Hendry. Then we got Matt Clarke the goalkeeper from Bradford on loan. Every day there was another challenge. Something else would turn up that would cause you a problem, and it wasn't simply about the football, though heaven knows the football side of the job creates enough problems in itself, but there would be one financial problem after another. That made it very difficult for everybody at the club to work. Effectively we were trying to build a successful business from one that was basically bust.'

Despite the changes to personnel, 2000 ended with Wanderers on a charge. On Boxing Day they beat Sheffield Wednesday 2–0 at the Reebok to make it five successive victories. By the time Allardyce and his troops went to Hillsborough for the return match at the end of January, they had been in the top two for eight weeks – only Fulham were ahead of them in the race for promotion. They won convincingly in South Yorkshire, 3–0, with goals from Ricardo Gardner, the prolific Ricketts and Ian Marshall.

At this stage of the season Wanderers were going up. Definitely.

But February was an unhappy month. A succession of draws meant that Blackburn Rovers were suddenly breathing down their necks. The month saw the club try a 'Fiver a Seat' initiative for a midweek match against Grimsby. It worked in one sense with more than 24,000 passing through the turnstiles, but it backfired in another. For Wanderers

Hero: Per Frandsen celebrates as Bolton fight back in the Play-off match at West Brom.

put on a disappointing display against a side struggling against relegation. The 2–2 draw was the side's third draw in five games against bottom six opposition. Dropping points so carelessly was starting to take its toll.

At this stage of the season Wanderers were going up. Possibly.

By now Fulham's waltz to the title was unstoppable. Second spot was the only thing to fight for and the scrap was fierce. Blackburn Rovers, who knocked Wanderers out of the FA Cup after a replay, were emerging as serious rivals to Bolton for the one remaining automatic promotion place. And as the tension started to grow

Wanderers' grip on second spot weakened. A run of successive home draws piled on the frustration. Bolton were stumbling; Rovers were relentless. At precisely the wrong stage of the season Wanderers went seven games without a Reebok win. They paid a heavy price. Automatic promotion went to their local rivals.

The home draw sequence was finally ended by a Dean Holdsworth winner, a cheeky 25-yard free-kick, against Norwich in April, but it was too little too late. Wanderers had to settle for the Play-offs.

At this stage of the season Wanderers were going up. Maybe.

On 13 May 2001 Wanderers went to West Brom for the first leg of the semi-final clash. Despite having finished 13 points ahead of Gary Megson's men, Wanderers were outplayed for the first hour at The Hawthorns, with Jason Roberts and Lee Hughes giving Albion a deserved 2–0 lead. Then with 10 minutes to go Bergsson headed home a Hansen corner to give Bolton a lifeline.

'All season we had been really determined to go one better than we had in the previous two years,' says Bergsson. 'Right from the start there was nothing else in the squad but a determination to get close to the 90-point mark. We didn't quite do it (they finished on 89) and we ended up in the Play-offs yet again. In the first leg at West Brom we had been playing terrible football. You couldn't complain about the scoreline at that point. We were 2–0 down and deserved to be. Then in the second half Per Frandsen came on and helped us change the game. Colin Hendry and myself started getting our act together at the back and things improved.

'Then with time running out I managed to get on the scoresheet. I think that is probably the most important goal of my career. Per then scored from the penalty spot and so we managed to pull it back to 2–2. We had somehow managed to pull it around just when our entire season was beginning to look like finishing in disappointment again.'

Four days later Wanderers completed the job. This time around there were no refereeing controversies or late dramas. Bergsson, Ricardo Gardner and Michael Ricketts completed a regulation 3–0 win over an utterly deflated West Brom.

Victory set up a Play-off Final clash with Preston North End at Cardiff's Millennium Stadium, and once again Wanderers had taken the season to the very last game. Dean Holdsworth says Wanderers went to Cardiff full of belief that they would triumph. 'There was absolutely no doubt in anybody's mind in the dressing room at the Millennium Stadium that we were going to win that day.'

Hopes turned into reality when Gareth Farrelly scored in the 17th minute. Of course, Ricketts had to get on the scoresheet and did towards the end with his 24th goal of the season. Then Gardner applied the finishing gloss with the third.

'I was so nervous before that match,' says Bergsson. 'We had come down to Cardiff full of belief that we should be able to beat

Dressing room celebrations after Bolton make it to the Play-off Final.

Preston. We proved it on the day. We were comfortable 3–0 winners, but it wasn't a particularly good game. Still it was a game we deserved to win, and we were back in the Premier League. The only question for me was whether I would carry on for another season. I had promised my wife Ella at the start of the season that it was just going to be one more year, but she had seen the game at Cardiff, and I think she knew in her heart that I wanted one more, and I wouldn't be able to say no if I was asked to carry on.'

A mere 19 months after being appointed Allardyce had guided Wanderers back into the top flight of English football and – despite the fact that the bookies reckoned he'd be taking them back down 12 months later – the club had hit the jackpot.

Wanderers were going up!

Going up: Michael Ricketts celebrates as Bolton beat Preston in the Play-off Final and book their return to the Premier League.

Ten Non-Wanderers Events at the Reebok Stadium

Oasis Concert (Music)

Coldplay Concert (Music)

Great Britain v New Zealand (Rugby League)

Amir Khan v Mario Kindelan (Boxing)

St Helens v Brisbane Broncos (Rugby League)

Elton John Concert (Music)

England v Brazil (Women's football international)

UK Open (Darts)

England v Yugoslavia (Under-21 International)

Lulu Concert (Music)

2000–01

Ins

Anthony Barness (Charlton Athletic), Simon Charlton (Birmingham City), Ian Marshall (Leicester City), Michael Ricketts (Walsall), Per Frandsen (Blackburn Rovers), Isiah Rankin (loan, Bradford City), Colin Hendry (Coventry City), Tommy Wright (Manchester City), Emmanuele Morini (Roma), Carsten Fredgaard (loan, FC Copenhagen), John Gope-Fenepej (loan, FC Lens), Matt Clarke (loan, Bradford City), Andy Campbell (loan, Middlesbrough), Leam Richardson (Blackburn Rovers), Jeff Smith (Bishop Auckland), Nicky Summerbee (Sunderland).

Outs

Eidur Gudjohnsen (Chelsea), Claus Jensen (Charlton), Michael Johansen (AB Copenhagen), Andy Campbell (loan, Middlesbrough), Frank Passi (retired), Jimmy Phillips (retired), Tommy Wright (Ballymena United), Carsten Fredgaard (loan, FC Copenhagen), Matt Clarke (loan, Bradford City).

Surprise Packages

Punted hopefully upfield, the ball came arrowing down out of the slate-grey Lancashire sky like a guided missile. Mere mortals would have tried to get out of its path for fear of injury. Most professional footballers might have attempted a header into the path of a colleague, but today was different. Today a football genius was waiting for the 'pass'.

Youri Djorkaeff didn't know fear on a football pitch. And Djorkaeff certainly didn't favour the hopeful flick-on. No, Youri was the exception because he was just that – an exceptional player. So with the ball flying towards him he instinctively got into a perfect position and delicately trapped it under his heel. Sorry, no, he didn't trap it, he caressed it. He brought it under his spell. And here's the best part. He did all of this wearing a Bolton Wanderers shirt.

Djorkaeff playing for Bolton. Sacre bleu! The supporters could hardly believe it. They bowed down in adulation, chanting 'We're not worthy' every time he jogged across to take a corner. But they weren't the only ones taken aback when Wanderers recruited him in February of the 2001–02 season.

The signing of Djorkaeff was the ultimate example of Wanderers daring to think big – but it was done with one eye on the lessons learned from their recent past. His short-term contract ensured there would be no lasting damage if the worst was to happen.

His arrival was also a triumph for the stadium itself. Put simply, no Reebok, no Youri.

'Without a shadow of doubt, we wouldn't have been as successful as we have been without the stadium,' says Allardyce. 'Without it we would never have seen the likes of Youri Djorkaeff in a Bolton Wanderers shirt. Imagine what would have happened if I had taken him down to Burnden Park and said 'This is where you are going to play.' I don't

French polish: World Cup winner Youri Djorkaeff in a Bolton Wanderers shirt.

think so. He never would have signed in a million years. Mind you, it was hard enough keeping players away from the training ground when we were trying to sign them. I couldn't take them there because we were working out of Portakabins.

'Whenever potential new signings asked about the training facilities, I used to say, "Don't worry about that, it's fine." Then afterwards they used to come and knock on my door and say "You never told me the training ground was like this," and I'd ask

"Well if you saw it was like this would you have signed on?" But the Reebok was different. It sold itself. When we were trying to improve the squad and attract better players it was as important in selling the club to them as the side being in the Premier League. The stadium may be compact in terms of capacity, but it was a state-of-the-art design. And to me it still looks as good today as it did when it was built. I think that's very important when something doesn't age very quickly.'

Allardyce had successfully secured promotion to the Premier League by clever use of the loan system, and he knew that without the financial muscle of his Premier League rivals he would have to repeat the trick if Bolton's stay in the top flight was going to last longer than one season.

When Wanderers beat Preston at Cardiff in May 2001 to clinch promotion they had been immediately installed as the bookies' favourites to be relegated. It was hard to question their logic. Play-off winners rarely prospered, and Bolton's two most recent jaunts in the Premier League in the 1990s had been strictly temporary.

Everyone knew that Bolton wouldn't be able to spend big in the transfer market to

Premier test: it is all smiles for Big Sam and Bolton legend Nat Lofthouse after the Play-off win at Cardiff, but the manager knew that staying up would be a real test.

strengthen the squad. It all pointed to a season-long slog at the wrong end of the table, hardly the sort of prospect likely to attract world-renowned names.

But for Allardyce reaching the Premier League was only the start. Ambitious in his own right, he wanted to manage consistently at the highest level. He was determined to keep Bolton up even if it meant taking on William Hill and Joe Coral as well as Messrs Ferguson and Wenger.

'From day one, I knew we needed a strategy for recruitment that no one else had thought of. My aim was to establish Bolton Wanderers in the Premier League. I knew I would only be able to do it by getting players with both talent and experience. My problem was that players with talent and experience in this country were already in the Premier League, and if we wanted them it was going to cost millions. Looking outside the Premier League was our only realistic option.'

What worked in his favour at the time was the financial situation at many of Europe's biggest clubs. Big spending in the late 90s had pushed several to the brink of ruin, and many clubs had overcrowded squads that they suddenly found they could no longer afford.

'At that time the likes of Barcelona, Juventus, Inter Milan and Real Madrid were struggling because the transfer market had stuttered. They had 45 or 50 players on their books, and they couldn't afford to keep them all. So we decided to use the loan system to its full potential.'

Allardyce had found the perfect hunting ground. The first player to come to his attention was defender Bruno N'Gotty. The French international had enjoyed multi-million pound moves around the continent, taking in Lyon, Paris Saint-Germain and AC Milan before showing up on the Allardyce radar at Marseille in the summer of 2001. By September a loan move to the Reebok until the end of the season had been agreed.

Wanderers managed to sign a player who had gone for more than £15 million in transfer fees for relatively little financial outlay – and, just as crucially to the board, with very little long-term risk. N'Gotty's transfer to Bolton became the template for how Wanderers would gain a foothold in the Premier League.

'N'Gotty was a player who was relatively unknown to the English game, but he had moved clubs for big money throughout his career before we brought him in on loan,' says chairman Phil Gartside. 'When he was at Marseille they were in danger of going bust

Loan star: defender Bruno N'Gotty, who arrived on loan.

so they had to offload players. We got him at a time when they hadn't paid his wages for several weeks. It was an opportune piece of business for us because we got our hands on a player of immense talent. N'Gotty stayed for five years and was a cornerstone for a lot of the things we did in that time.'

The deal fit in with Wanderers' business plan too. 'When we were promoted to the Premier League our strategy was to budget to finish 17th,' says chief executive Allan Duckworth. 'We called it Downside Risk Management. It was our attempt to ensure the club would be in good shape if we were to go down. We certainly weren't suddenly going to spend money that we didn't have. So we adopted a strategy of trying to build a squad that had a core of young players like Jussi Jaaskelainen, Ricardo Gardner and Kevin Nolan. These were players we were prepared to give longer-term contracts to. We then identified another group of more experienced players who were on short-term contracts or loans. Then we had the stars who we brought in on loan like Bruno N'Gotty, who would not be here if we went down. We knew that if we were relegated we would be left with a core of younger players that we

could build around and start again. Having a strategy in place like that helped to give the bank confidence too. At the same time the hotel was starting to help make ends meet too.'

Despite the loan plan, the manager always knew that the Premier League would provide a tough test for his team – players and backroom staff. Allardyce was also fully aware that it was vital for Wanderers to get off to a good start if they were going to achieve their ultimate goal – survival.

They didn't. They got off to a magnificent start!

On the opening day of the season, Saturday 18 August 2001, Allardyce took his side to Leicester City. They produced the most talked-about result of the day: a thumping 5–0 victory. They then followed that up with victories in their first two games

First day glory: Kevin Nolan runs over to the Bolton fans at Leicester as Wanderers mark their Premier League return in style.

Taking the Michael: Anthony Barness congratulates scorer Michael Ricketts as Bolton romp to a 5–0 win at Leicester.

at the Reebok – beating Middlesbrough 1–0 and then Liverpool 2–1. The latter came from a last-minute Dean Holdsworth goal courtesy of a gaffe by Liverpool 'keeper Sander Westerveld. Three games, maximum points and Wanderers were top of the League!

A draw at Leeds United kept them there and took the side's points tally into double figures, but then reality set in. Despite, proving to be well organised and difficult to beat, Wanderers went six games without a win.

Few gave them a hope when they went to Old Trafford in October to take on the reigning Premier League champions Manchester United. When Argentine

Hold up: Wanderers go top of the table thanks to Dean Holdsworth's winner against Liverpool.

Man-eater: Michael Ricketts shoots past Fabian Barthez to give Bolton victory at Old Trafford against Manchester United.

Scorer Ricketts runs to the Bolton supporters, who go wild.

Bolton fans celebrate.

international Juan Veron put United 1–0 ahead in the 25th minute it looked like being a long and uncomfortable afternoon for Bolton. But 10 minutes later N'Gotty played a ball up to Michael Ricketts on the edge of the United area. He headed it into the path of Kevin Nolan who volleyed past Fabian Barthez to put Wanderers on level terms at the break. And the unthinkable happened six minutes from time when Ricketts robbed Wes Brown and powered a drive past Barthez to set up a famous Bolton victory.

Ricketts, who had also scored in the opener at Leicester, was taking to the Premier League with ease. Despite the step up in class there was no sign of a dip in his phenomenal form.

'It was good to play on massive stages,' says Ricketts. 'We had a good set of players but not a great deal of strength in depth in the squad. But we set a goal of trying to stay in the Premier League and tried to achieve that together. We spurred one another on.

'I am always confident in my abilities, but I was scoring goals regularly too, which helps. Every player dreams of playing at stadiums like Old Trafford and Anfield, and it was wonderful to be part of that. Some of the lads had played in the Premier League before, but there were a few of us who had never been there. For us it was all new and exciting.

'As for the game at Old Trafford it is all just a blur. I remember the win and I remember Kevin Nolan's goal more than my own.'

The Ricketts story was pure Roy of the Rovers stuff. Less than 18 months after leaving Walsall, the striker was being touted as a potential England international and Allardyce was leading the fan club. The Ricketts rise to fame reached its peak in February. After making his case with 15 goals for Wanderers, he was selected for his country. He was given a 45 minute run-out against Holland in Amsterdam, though cut a relatively anonymous figure.

'Though it was a step up I didn't get too worried about it,' says Ricketts. 'I felt it was a natural progression. I was scoring goals in a decent side so for me it was just another challenge. Every step up is harder. Don't let anyone tell you there is no difference. You are playing against better players in every team, players who have cost a lot of money and who have a lot of experience. I learned a lot during my time at Bolton because I worked with a top-class manger, great coaches and great players.'

But Bolton's stunning victory at Old Trafford turned out to be the high water mark of the League campaign. The side managed just one win in their next 15 games and, to add insult to injury, weakened Wanderers teams were knocked out of both the FA Cup and League Cup by Tottenham. In truth, they were hammered 4–0 in the FA Cup and 6–0 in the League Cup. Allardyce was even accused by some in the media of disrespecting the FA Cup because of his team selections. He defended his choices by pointing out that his priority was Premier League survival.

Despite a lack of victories, Allardyce was reasonably content with the first half of the season.

'We had seen from our research that a lot of newly-promoted sides generally lose heavily on at least three or four occasions by more than three goals. So we kind of accepted that was going to be the case. Naturally we tried our very best to prevent it and that season, while we had some heavy defeats, we very rarely lost more than two games on the trot. That was significant because we were making sure that confidence levels didn't suffer too much.'

Wanderers may have been sliding dangerously down the table, but a measure of the fighting spirit in the squad came in the return game against Leicester City at the Reebok on 29 December.

Allardyce describes the match as 'one of the most bizarre results there has ever been at the club.' Bolton were reduced to nine men after just 23 minutes when referee Mike Riley sent off Paul Warhurst and Dean Holdsworth for challenges on Robbie Savage. Not surprisingly, given the body count,

War games: Mike Riley shows Paul Warhurst the red card early in the game against Leicester.

Riley saying something: Dean Holdsworth goes the same way as Warhurst as referee Riley reduces Bolton to nine men.

Savage treatment: Leicester's Robbie Savage fumes about being substituted after being involved in both dismissals.

Wanderers found themselves 2–0 down with less than half an hour gone. By coincidence, this particular match had been selected by the producers of an ITV documentary looking at the stresses felt by football managers. Both Allardyce and his Leicester counterpart Dave Bassett had agreed to wear heart monitors for the 90 minutes.

Despite the odds being stacked heavily against them, Bolton's players came storming back.

'The sending offs had upset the lads so much that in work rate alone they went over and above what they would ever normally do,' says Allardyce. 'They ran for one and a half men on that day. In the end it brought a result. An incredible result. We sneaked a goal back through Kevin Nolan before half-time, which gave the lads the lift they needed. I really didn't need to encourage them too much at half-time. They were so wound up about the sendings off and the decisions that were going against them that it was more a case of trying to get them just to listen to the tactics for the second half.'

In the event referee Riley evened the balance a little in the second half when he sent off Leicester's Muzzy Izzet for two yellow-card offences. But it looked as though the never-saydie attitude of the 'Bolton Nine' would be in vain as the clock ticked down. Then four minutes into injury time the unstoppable Ricketts headed past Ian Walker in the Leicester goal to give Wanderers the most unlikely draw.

'There is no better time to score when you're down to nine men than the last kick of a game because the opposition don't have any time to come back against you,' says Allardyce. The TV programme later showed that Big Sam's heart monitor peaked when Ricketts scored his late goal.

To get a point in such desperate circumstances was great, but the significant thing for the manager was the courage his players had displayed.

'That one performance told me that we were not going to be relegated that season. It showed we had the spirit to survive. I remember in the dressing room after the game I told the players that it would be a catalyst for us staying in the Premier League. I knew that if we could retain that spirit and level of commitment we could stay up.'

N'Gotty's signing aside, Allardyce had more or less kept faith with the side that had won promotion. However, as the season progressed it became increasingly obvious to Allardyce

that he needed an injection of new blood. And once again he turned to the loan market. In January he persuaded German international striker Fredi Bobic to come on loan from Borussia Dortmund. Bobic was happy for the chance to impress national coach Rudi Voeller ahead of that summer's World Cup in Japan and South Korea. That same month Danish defensive midfielder Stig Tofting arrived from SV Hamburg, also on loan, and also with one eye on the World Cup. Both fit the Bolton criteria. Both were experienced internationals and quality players.

But Allardyce's next move was his most daring. Chairman Phil Gartside remembers taking a call in February 2002.

'Sam rang me out of the blue and said, 'I've got a chance to take Djorkaeff'. I said, 'Rubbish, you're having me on!' But he was deadly serious so I told him to chase it and see whether he could pull it off. Allardyce went over to Germany to meet Djorkaeff and, after showing off all his silver-tongued skills, returned to the Reebok with a World Cup winner in tow!

'It was fantastic. I think it was a sign to the outside world that we were ready to take the next step.'

Fred carpet: German international Fredi Bobic on his Bolton debut against Chelsea at the Reebok.

National service: Tough tackling Stig Tofting arrived at Bolton hoping to earn a World Cup place for Denmark.

In Germany Allardyce had found an unhappy Djorkaeff. Having fallen out with Kaiserslautern coach Andreas Brehme, Djorkaeff was desperate for a move. Like Bobic and Tofting, he too had the World Cup very much in his thoughts. At 33, Djorkaeff already had a World Cup-winners' medal from 1998, as well as a 2000 European Championship-winners' medal with France, but he knew that without games he would have no chance of making the French squad for the 2002 tournament.

With Youri desperate for one final hoorah, Allardyce's timing was perfect.

'Sam flew out to see me and told me all about the club and their plans,' said Djorkaeff. 'Because of my situation at Kaiserslautern and because of the World Cup that summer, I wanted to move. West Ham and Aston Villa were also in contact with my agent, but I had to make a quick decision because the World Cup was getting close. Bolton was the one club that really interested me, simply because they were the most interested in me. From a financial point of view, it was probably not the best deal available, but it was the best deal for me at that time.

'I found what Sam wanted to do with the club very exciting. It was a challenge but it was great to have something to fight for. He told me that he wanted to turn Bolton into a top club, which is actually what he managed to do. Though at that point his short-term goal was to keep Bolton in the Premier League for two successive seasons.

'He also told me that he wanted to be in charge of a big club – not what Bolton was at

the time, but what it has become since then. He asked me to help.

'I guess I was a big name that people could recognise and that in itself gave the club a certain amount of credibility. Sam also told me that the team would play for me, and they would more or less give me the keys to the shop. I was a little bit surprised, but it was refreshing to hear this after my time in Germany had ended so badly.'

Along with his international honours, Djorkaeff, whose father Jean had been a regular right-back for the French national side in the 1960s, was no stranger to club success.

He arrived at the Reebok with a host of medals, among them the Cup-winners' Cup with Paris Saint-Germain (1996) and the UEFA Cup with Inter Milan (1998). Fighting for survival was going to be an entirely new experience.

'It was the first time in the whole of my career that I had been involved in a relegation battle. It was very tough. Every goal, every tackle and every point was crucial. I felt I had a lot of responsibility for the team. For me, having been involved in both title battles and survival fights, it is much easier to fight for championships than it is to be in a relegation scrap. That's very difficult. Every match was important.

'When I arrived I was really fresh and it was great to give confidence to the rest of the players. I think that was one of my key contributions. I managed to give confidence to the players.'

Convincing Djorkaeff to join the fray was a major coup for a club of Bolton's stature and it did more than simply improve the Wanderers playing squad. Sports psychologist Mike Forde explains 'Youri was a very pivotal guy to the value of this club. He altered the whole standing of the club overnight because he changed the way people thought about Bolton Wanderers – both insiders and outsiders. The very fact that we'd managed to bring a guy of his status, a World Cup winner, to little old Bolton was a massive milestone.'

Chief executive Allan Duckworth agrees that the deal was a masterstroke from Allardyce. 'When Sam spotted the opportunity to bring in Djorkaeff he saw it as a two-fold thing,' says Duckworth. 'He knew Youri was a fantastic footballer, but Sam also saw him as a magnet to attract other players to

the club. So it was quite a clever signing in that sense – because there were two big benefits.'

If financially the deal wasn't the best a player of Djorkaeff's talents could have expected, it was certainly the best the club could come up with at the time.

Says Gartside, 'To be honest we really went out on a limb for Djorkaeff because we actually provided him with a service. We employed people at great expense, for salaries that people could only dream of, just to look after him. That was on top of his own salary. We did things we hadn't done before as a club. We had people to chauffeur him, people to look after him if he had a problem, to take his wife shopping and to look after his kids.'

That said, Djorkaeff wasn't simply expected to contribute for 90 minutes on a Saturday afternoon. The backroom staff, and Allardyce in particular, picked his brain and examined the experiences he had been through at other clubs to see if there was anything Bolton could learn from.

'Youri was one of a kind. He was a very bright guy,' says Forde. 'I asked him about his World Cup experiences in part because I was genuinely interested, but also to see if we could take anything from them. And certainly he played a part in helping us develop the training ground at Euxton. Youri was important because he guided us in terms of what we needed to put in there. You could say he helped to mould us.

'If you say, for example, that the average player earns £1 million a year then their home is going to be of a certain standard. But their second home is the training ground. It's where a lot of time is spent on a regular basis. However, when Youri first arrived our training ground was not what you'd call an inspirational place to be.

'So I sat down with him and asked what was required to help make him feel inspired. I wanted to know what he wanted to see when he drove through the gates. Youri was a very good person to ask because he was very bright, his English was very good, and throughout his career, at club and international level, he'd been around excellence. Youri knew what a winning environment looked like, and he knew a winning team. He wanted to do well at Bolton on an individual level because of his World Cup ambitions, but he was also eager to add something to the environment. I think

that being part of that also helped keep him motivated.'

His signing wasn't totally risk free. Rightly or wrongly, Djorkaeff came to Bolton with a tarnished reputation. He had fallen out with his previous coach which left a question mark over his temperament, but Allardyce describes the Frenchman as a model professional.

'Youri was one of the fittest and most dedicated players I've ever come across,' says Allardyce. 'Dedication is one of the most crucial areas for any Premier League footballer. They are not allowed to go astray at all these days. It's a really hard life. You get paid handsomely for it, but it's incredibly difficult, a life full of commitment.

'They have to commit to the training regime. They have to commit to eating sensibly. They have to commit to watching their weight, to keeping their body fat low, to watching their body mass. They have to commit to the speed training, the flexibility exercises, the mobility training, the skill levels. They have to develop an understanding of how the team has to play, the tactical awareness and so on.

'They even have to know the level of rest and sleep that's needed. That can become very, very boring, particularly when your friends are doing something you can't. Life as a Premier League footballer is not as easy as some people think. When you are a young man you are bubbling with energy, but you have to conserve it. Without that dedication both physically and mentally you will fall by the wayside, and we have seen enough examples of that in football over the years.

'If you're a natural then it's not quite as bad, and Youri Djorkaeff was a natural. He was naturally talented and a naturally fit player. He is just wired that way. He could have three weeks off and play like he'd never been away. There are very few players in the world of football who are capable of that, but that's why he was world class. But although he was lucky to be blessed with so much natural talent he also worked as hard as anyone I have ever come across.'

When Djorkaeff arrived at Bolton he joined a side in desperate need of a boost. Wins were harder and harder to come by and the slide down the table was inexorable. By February, a 3–2 defeat at Newcastle had seen Wanderers slip into the bottom three for the first time that season. The defeat at St James' Park will be remembered by Bolton fans for

referee David Elleray's decision to penalise Jussi Jaaskelainen for holding onto the ball longer than six seconds. Needless to say Alan Shearer scored from the resulting free-kick.

Bolton then received a much-needed lift thanks to a 1–0 victory over West Ham at the Reebok in Tofting's debut game.

Djorkaeff made his bow at Southampton in a 0–0 draw, then made his Reebok debut in a 1–1 draw against Blackburn Rovers, who had also been dragged into the relegation scrap. Three games unbeaten represented a revival of sorts.

However, successive defeats at Sunderland and at home to Derby County put Wanderers back in the drop zone and, with Bobic failing to fire in front of goal, the wisdom of Allardyce's loan signings was being called into question in some quarters.

The doubters were silenced in mid-March when Djorkaeff inspired a 2–1 victory at Charlton. He scored both Wanderers goals, the first from the edge of the box after good work from Bobic and the second from a free-kick that took a deflection. It was enough to earn Wanderers their first away win for more than four months. It was followed up by a thrilling 3–2 victory over Aston Villa at the

Bob slayer: Fredi Bobic is congratulated by Youri Djorkaeff after giving Bolton the lead in their must-win game against relegation rivals Ipswich.

Reebok in which Bobic finally broke his duck. Those six points had given Wanderers the edge in what was a desperate relegation scrap.

Next up at the Reebok was Ipswich for a game that was every bit as important as the clubs' recent Play-off meetings. Ipswich had surprised a lot of people by finishing in fifth place the season before. But this season George Burley's side had struggled to cope with the twin demands of the Premier League and UEFA Cup. They arrived at Bolton occupying the third relegation spot, four points adrift of Wanderers.

Their plight was made worse by a run-in which had them facing the combined might of Manchester United, Arsenal and Liverpool in three of their last four matches. Not the games you'd chose if your survival depended on them.

So the Tractor Boys arrived at the Reebok knowing they really needed to take something out of the game.

Net profit: Djorkaeff and Wallace both celebrate as Bobic (hidden) scores his third and Bolton's fourth to seal the points against Ipswich.

If ever there was a match for the Allardyce loan stars to live up to their high-class reputations this was it. They didn't let him down. With just over a minute played, Bobic killed a long-range effort from Gardner with his heel, swivelled and shot past Ipswich 'keeper Andy Marshall. Nerves were settled. Then for the rest of the first half Wanderers were rampant. The German headed a second on 30 minutes, then turned provider for Djorkaeff moments later. Bobic still had time

to flick home a Gardner corner to make it 4–0 and complete a hat-trick before the half-time whistle! Although Ipswich pulled one back before the death, the result all but condemned them.

Allardyce's quest to keep Wanderers in the top flight for two successive seasons was effectively complete with four games left to play. A 1–1 draw at the Reebok against Tottenham took them to the magic 40-point mark, and when Ipswich lost to Manchester

United in their penultimate game of the season it was mission accomplished.

Djorkaeff's inspirational displays that helped secure the club's survival weren't his only legacy.

'We learned an awful lot from Youri,' says Allardyce. 'If you don't learn from people like him, if you don't ask him about his first-hand experiences, it's a real waste. But I am not sure that a lot of managers and coaches do it. We sat down with Youri and asked him about his experiences. We asked him what conditions were like at previous clubs like Milan and Kaiserslautern. What were the training facilities like? What are the Germans like compared to the Italians, compared to the French? If you don't ask you don't find out. It was a great learning experience for us.

'We basically said to him "You like what we do, so tell us from your experience what we could do that will make us better." We asked him what were the things that inspired him and what allowed him to produce at a high level. Then we tried to see if there was something in those experiences we could use. Some of it cost millions, some of it cost nothing, only the human touch.

'For example, we had brought all these foreign players into the club, and we wondered whether we should change the way we prepared for games. We thought that maybe they would prefer to be taken away on Thursday and Friday like they do in Italy. But Youri said he hated every minute of that. He told us he much preferred our approach. We let him stay at home until the morning of games, which meant he could spend more time with his family relaxing.

'Personally, I agree. Sat in a hotel bedroom has got to be the worst place to be to prepare for a game. I hate it. I often take a sleeping pill just to get to sleep.'

Djorkaeff too enjoyed the relationship with the Wanderers manager and appreciated being asked for his input into so many aspects of the club.

'Every day Sam and I talked and it was very nice for me to feel he was listening. We used to be able talk man to man. I could tell him if I wasn't happy with say the food or the training facilities because he knew it was not a case of me being unhappy for myself. Sam would ask "Is the gym good?" or "Is the training OK?" and it was a case of explaining things for the good of the club and the good of the team as a whole. I was talking about

Safe bet: 'keeper Jussi Jaaskelainen, pictured making a save from Arsenal's Freddie Ljungberg, was one of the heroes of the Bolton campaign.

what we did here and how it compared to Inter, for example. It was interesting. We enjoyed just talking about football.

'I also enjoyed being part of the club. Bolton had a proper family feel and the relationship I had with them all was very interesting. That's why I decided to come back to the club after the World Cup. I felt that it was a family. We were very close. At that point I could have gone to several other clubs, but I felt that we were at the start of something at Bolton.

'I also enjoyed the "kick and rush" of the English game,' laughs Youri. 'I enjoyed the commitment in each and every game at the

Reebok. Those three o'clock matches on a Saturday afternoon were worth all the sweat and hard work that we put in every day in training. I'm not surprised by the success the club is now having. Each and every year they've taken a step forward and brought in good players and they're now a tough team, very tough to beat, with the right spirit and the right mentality.'

For Allardyce Djorkaeff's decision to return to the Reebok was a surprise but a very welcome one. It spoke volumes about the Reebok revolution he was trying to effect.

'Youri came to us initially because he wanted to play in the World Cup, and because of his performances for us he was selected by France. Initially he had planned to retire after the World Cup, but then he rang me up and said "Can I come back? I enjoyed what I did."

'He actually wanted to come back and play for us even if that meant being involved in another struggle for another season!

'The fact he wanted to come back was effectively him saying that what we were doing was right. We must have been doing things behind the scenes that he enjoyed.

'We were putting a lot of time and research into finding a way to take the club to the next level after survival. And Youri was one of the key elements at the start of the entire process because he bought into it straight away.'

Best 10 Games at the Reebok Stadium

Bolton Wanderers 5–2 Crystal Palace, 2 February 1998

Bolton Wanderers 2–1 Middlesbrough, 11 May 2003

Bolton Wanderers 5–2 Aston Villa, 21 January 2004

Bolton Wanderers 4–1 Charlton, 14 August 2004

Bolton Wanderers 3–2 Everton, 15 May 2005

Bolton Wanderers 3–0 West Brom, 17 May 2001

Bolton Wanderers 2–2 Leicester, 29 December 01

Bolton Wanderers 4–3 Newcastle, 26 December 2002

Bolton Wanderers 2–2 Arsenal, 26 April 03

Bolton Wanderers 4–1 Ipswich, 6 April 2002

2001–02
Ins
Henrik Pedersen (Silkeborg), Rod Wallace (Glasgow Rangers), Bruno N'Gotty (loan, Olympique Marseille), Jermaine Johnson (Tivoli Gardens), Akinori Nishizawa (loan, Cerezo Osaka), Fredi Bobic (loan, Borussia Dortmund), Youri Djorkaeff (Kaiserslautern), Stig Tofting (SV Hamburg), Djibril Diawara (loan, Torino), Mario Espartero (loan, FC Metz), Kostas Konstantinos (loan, Hertha Berlin), Kevin Poole (Birmingham City), Nicky Southall (Gillingham).
Outs
Fredi Bobic (loan, Borussia Dortmund), Dean Holden (Oldham Athletic), Kostas Konstantinos (loan, Hertha Berlin), Ian Marshall (Blackpool), Emmanuelle Morini (Panahaiki), Akinori Nishizawa (loan, Cerezo Osaka), Nicky Summerbee (Manchester City), Djibril Diawara (loan, Torino).

Natural Born Footballer

There are days when a trip to a football match is just part of a weekly routine – work, gym, telly, pub, footy. Then there are the games that take over your life. It's your first thought when you wake up. Even before you have taken your first sip of coffee you've played out every potential outcome in your head. The coffee doesn't taste right because you get that sick-in-the-stomach feeling just thinking about 'The Game'. The League table is studied more intently then any exam paper and permutations of all the possible results and points tallies are analysed over and over.

You're 45 and all of a sudden you're 15 again – it's that good!

April 2003. The season is reaching boiling point and two of the three relegation places looked done and dusted.

By this point of the campaign not even the SAS could save a free-falling Sunderland. Howard Wilkinson and Mick McCarthy had both tried and failed to revive the Black Cats'

fortunes following the October sacking of Peter Reid, a one-time Wanderers teammate of Sam Allardyce.

Joining them for the fall were West Bromwich Albion. They'd shown a little more faith in Gary Megson. Their team was pragmatic if a little short on flair and survival in the big League was proving too tough.

By 19 April the only question mark at the wrong end of the table was over the third and final place in the drop zone. What wasn't in doubt was that the unwanted berth would go to either West Ham United or Bolton Wanderers. So the stakes could hardly have been much higher when the Hammers visited the Reebok that day. Wanderers went into the game with a slight edge. With five games to go they led the Londoners by a slender three points.

Conventional wisdom suggested that what you needed in a relegation dogfight were the kind of terrier-like players the British game

The natural: Nigerian star Jay Jay Okocha, in action here against West Ham, played a starring role in the 2002–03 season.

thrived on. Cool cats with more tricks than Paul Daniels were frowned upon in such desperate situations.

Big Sam, however, had other ideas. For in Bolton's hour of need he had put his faith in one of the most outrageous talents to grace the football world during the previous decade.

He turned to Jay Jay.

Born on 14 August 1973, Augustine Azuka

Okocha – the Jay Jay bit came later – was brought up in Enugu, once Nigeria's coal capital.

By 2003 its most famous export was Okocha, but he mined an altogether different natural seam. His gift was football, and as soon as he could walk he had a ball at his feet. He truly was a natural-born talent.

'As a young boy I took every opportunity I got to play football. It was all I ever wanted to do. I started playing as soon as I could walk because I came from a football-playing family. There was always plenty of encouragement from my friends and family. We played in the streets where I was brought up and anything round got used for a ball.

'I've got two brothers and we all played football together all the time. Emmanuel is four years older than me, and I looked up to him. He was a midfielder and was very, very skilful. It's always nice to see your brother do what you want to do. But it was my aim to try and be better than him. It was a challenge.'

Okocha honed his skills on scorched earth pitches, playing for pleasure among the boys from the neighbourhood trying to emulate his brother.

Looking back Okocha's arrival on the world scene seems as natural as breathing. Anyone who has seen him with a ball at his feet knows he was blessed with an outrageous amount of ability. But incredibly the Nigerian was discovered almost by accident.

As a shy 16-year-old he went on a school trip to Germany. While he was there he was given a trial for Third Division Neunkirchen. Not surprisingly, they liked what they saw.

'When I got to Germany to see my friend I was asked to train with his team,' says Jay Jay. 'They offered to sign me there and then

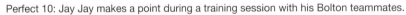
Perfect 10: Jay Jay makes a point during a training session with his Bolton teammates.

and that's how my career started. At that point in my life I had never thought that I would make it big. Then I suddenly saw that I had a good opportunity of making football my profession, so I grabbed it.

'It was an exciting time to be in Germany because the national team had just won the World Cup (Italia '90). As a football fanatic I was really interested to see how football was played there, and I jumped at the chance. Living away from home for the first time was very difficult but my love of football kept me going. I knew this was a big opportunity for me.

'Of course, sometimes I felt like going back but, as a kid, you like to be on your own and prove to yourself that you can do things. In the end I was determined to stick with it. For me it was all about football. I wasn't bothered about where I played. It was easy because football is a special language.'

And thus his school trip became the launch pad for an incredible football career.

Off the field Okocha is a quietly spoken family man – but put him on a football pitch and he's a showman. It's one thing playing keepy-uppy in the park with a few mates, it's quite another doing it in the middle of a blood-and-thunder Premier League match in front of several thousand. Few can display that kind of flair under pressure. But there have been few men born to match Okocha. Forget Bending it like Beckham at a free-kick and try juggling like Jay Jay when a defender is hacking at your ankles.

Not surprisingly, the young Okocha made waves with the small-town German club and after just one season there was plucked from relative obscurity and ushered into the big time when scouts from Bundesliga outfit Eintracht Frankfurt spotted his raw potential. In 1992 he signed his first ever professional contract.

Still just a teenager and a long way from home, there was a question mark over whether Okocha would manage the transition to the big time. He answered that in his first season with a goal against Karlsruher that's still talked about today. The magician went on an incredible dribble that took him almost the full length of the field before scoring. Jay Jay had arrived.

Thanks to TV, the Bundesliga was a global stage for the African's talents, and after four years in Germany Okocha was offered the chance to go to Turkey and play for Fenerbahce in a £1 million transfer.

By now he was also a regular in the Nigerian national side and starred in the 1996 Olympic Games. In Turkey Okocha's reputation continued to blossom. Thirty goals in just 61 games earned him adoration from the fanatical Fenerbahce supporters – adoration which at times became a little too hot for him to handle.

'The fans in England and in France are a lot more respectful. But in Turkey they are a lot more fanatical and just want to hug and kiss you so much all the time. In the end I had to run away from them.'

Following a series of dazzling displays for Nigeria in the French World Cup of 1998, Okocha was given the chance to leave the frenzied atmosphere of Fenerbahce behind. He became the most expensive African player in history when Paris Saint-Germain paid the Turkish side more than £9 million for his genius. He announced his arrival in French football with a stunning goal on his debut – Jay Jay doesn't do tap-ins.

But over time things didn't go as planned at PSG, and after four years Okocha was back on the market. At 28 and still at the peak of his powers, Okocha's talents were naturally coveted throughout the football world. In Nigeria his status was assured after proving his talents in club football in Germany, Turkey and France and on national service for his country.

It was during the World Cup of 2002 that word filtered back home to the UK that Okocha's next move would be to the Premier League.

News that Okocha was moving to one of the best Leagues in the world may not have rocked football, but his destination certainly did. For while TV money had made the Premier League a well-established magnet for foreign stars, the fact that Wanderers had got in ahead of the likes of Manchester United, Liverpool, Chelsea and Arsenal for one of the game's superstar players was little short of breathtaking.

Like the Djorkaeff deal a few months earlier, the move was orchestrated by Allardyce. The difference was that, while Djorkaeff was coming to the end of his playing days when he joined Bolton, Okocha was still at his peak.

His capture was greeted by a mixture of glee and disbelief among Wanderers fans – who suddenly found they had a new supporters' club branch in Enngu.

While Bolton fans were still pinching themselves, the pundits were already sharpening the knives. Questions were immediately raised about whether he would struggle to adapt to the pace and physical nature of the Premier League. Others wondered how long he would be happy at Bolton after a career spent hogging the limelight across continents.

But Allardyce wasn't prepared to let outside opinions of the club's status dent his own ambitions. He wanted to smash the club's 'little old Bolton' tag. He wasn't content managing a club of plucky but ultimately unsuccessful underdogs. Having survived in the Premier League, he wanted to build the playing squad's ability and experience in order to take Wanderers to the next level.

Like Djorkaeff before him, the experience of playing in a team struggling against relegation was a new one for Okocha. And, although well travelled, he had only been to England a couple of times before arriving at the Reebok in the summer of 2002.

'It was the first time I had played in English football, and I honestly didn't realise what the atmosphere would be like. Of course, I had seen matches on TV and people had tried to warn me about it, but until I experienced the incredible noise of the Reebok on matchdays I couldn't believe it. I am just glad I was lucky enough to experience it during my career.

'Before coming to Bolton I had been used to playing in teams that were battling for championships and medals. Joining a club that knew it would be battling against relegation was something new for me. It was different. I had to adjust to it, and I also had to adjust to playing in a team that lost quite a few games. That was a new experience too. But when I signed for the club I knew what I was letting myself in for.

'When I first spoke to Mr Allardyce he told me that he was keen to take the club up to another level and said he needed me to help achieve that. Thankfully, by the time I had left we had achieved what we had set out to.'

Okocha wasn't an instant hit. His debut on the opening day of the 2002–03 season at Fulham lasted till half-time when Wanderers were already 3–1 down.

The frantic pace and physical nature of the Premier League takes some getting used to, and though there were flashes of brilliance from the Nigerian in the early part of the season they were only fleeting. But the manager never lost faith in Jay Jay. He and Okocha shared a bond of mutual respect.

Says Jay Jay, 'At the beginning the boss said he wanted to bring me to the club to increase the side's ball possession and our ability to win games. Then over time we started to improve the squad and bring more players – better quality players – and my role in the side changed a little.'

Wanderers under Allardyce were known for being tactically shrewd, well organised, and difficult to beat. Despite that they still managed to find a way to accommodate a mercurial talent like Jay Jay.

'Sometimes it was frustrating for me to play in Sam's particular system, but then it wasn't about Jay Jay Okocha, it was about Bolton Wanderers, and I understood that. He had to develop a style that did not just suit one player but a style that would make the whole team successful, and you can't argue with what he has done. The system we developed as a team (incorporating the Okocha long throw as a serious weapon) was our way of being successful.

'We knew that if we went out on the attack against a team like Arsenal or Manchester United then we would struggle, but we also knew that we could sometimes out-battle sides like them.

'We had to play to our strengths. Sometimes that limited me and sometimes I couldn't play the way I would have loved, but I had to think about the team – we all had to think about the team.

'I think Sam's approach to players was very good. He knew what we wanted, and we knew what he wanted. The challenge was there. From a player's point of view, if you were being well treated it was natural to want to pay him back and try to get the results for him.'

If Bolton fans had thought that life in the Premier League would be a doddle after the successful relegation battle of 2001–02 then they were in for a nasty surprise. The only real bright spot came at Old Trafford when Kevin Nolan scored a late winner against United. A win at the Reebok in September over Aston Villa courtesy of a Michael Ricketts penalty was a rare victory in the first half of the season. Supporters had to wait nearly four months for another at the Reebok.

By November Wanderers had become rooted to the bottom of the table.

Déjà vu: Kevin Nolan scores as Bolton win at Manchester United for the second successive season.

They then produced a surprise 4–2 win at Leeds and followed that up with a few battling draws. That run of good form meant it was West Ham fans rather than Wanderers supporters who spent the festive period reading the 'Bottom at Christmas' headlines.

The side may have gone several weeks without a Reebok victory, but when one finally arrived it was worth waiting for. Bolton beat Newcastle United 4–3 in a breathless Boxing Day encounter in front of more than 27,000. Any victory at this stage was vital, but this one in particular sticks in the memory of Wanderers fans as it signalled the emergence of Okocha as a lethal weapon.

He set the side on the way to victory after

Boxing clever: Okocha scores as Bolton win a Boxing Day thriller against Newcastle.

just five minutes with a thunderbolt strike that became his trademark. More than that, however, Okocha appeared to be getting over his period of Premier League adjustment. This match didn't pass him by as earlier ones had. This time he was at its hub, orchestrating the action.

As the Spring arrived Okocha flourished. In February he turned in a step-over masterclass against Manchester United at the

Campo fires: Wanderers brought Ivan Campo, pictured scoring against Liverpool in September, from Real Madrid at the start of the 2002–03 season.

To Elland back: a Wanderers fan manages to disguise his glee as Bolton notch a surprise 4–2 win at Leeds in November.

Magic touch: Okocha turned in a masterclass as Bolton took on Manchester United at the Reebok.

Dance craze: Okocha and Bernard Mendy do a dance of delight as Bolton beat Spurs 1–0 at the Reebok.

Reebok that was as audacious as it was effective. But for an injury time Ole Gunnar Solskjaer equaliser, Okocha may have been the architect of a Wanderers win over their wealthy neighbours.

But the season's struggle for survival moved tortuously on. Points were accumulated at an agonisingly slow rate. A quick glance at the Premier League table was enough for most fans – it rarely looked healthy from a Bolton complexion.

It was a marathon quest for survival. But as Wanderers were continually cross-examined the irrepressible Okocha kept coming up with the answers.

Against Spurs at the Reebok in March the game was heading for stalemate when Djorkaeff was brought down in the last minute and Bolton were awarded a penalty. With nails being bitten all around him, Okocha coolly stepped up to try to claim the three points. All live on TV. Could he do it? Would he do it? Of course he did.

In fact, he scored it with a swagger that suggested the goal was never in doubt. Not only that, he then celebrated with a cheeky little dance inspired by something he had seen earlier on the TV sitcom *Friends*! You could almost hear the groans from East London as Okocha danced in the Winter Hill darkness.

A week later against Manchester City and Okocha started the game looking drained by his inspirational efforts. Maybe the weight of carrying a team was getting to him. Maybe Wanderers had exhausted their talisman. After 30 minutes he missed a penalty. The swagger had disappeared. However, what might have proved a shattering miss became his inspiration. It was as if someone had flicked Okocha's inner-switch to reawaken the super-galactic footballer within.

To say he made up for the spot-kick aberration would be like saying Muhammad Ali was a bit handy with his fists. For in the next 60 minutes Okocha was unstoppable. In

a blur of action he ran the show, setting up the opening goal and playing the rest of the game as though he and the ball were connected by a kind of supernatural force.

It finished Wanderers 2 City 0. At the final whistle the Reebok was acclaiming Wanderers' third successive win. The side had defied the pundits and taken 14 points out of 21. And the difference was Jay Jay. When Okocha had come to the party, hope had replaced despair.

No one was getting carried away. The situation was still seriously uncomfortable and defeat at Stamford Bridge a week after the City celebration only served to underline the precarious nature of Wanderers' hopes. In just seven days the mood had swung from happiness back to horror, from party to panic.

Safety was in sight, and yet Wanderers still had one foot among the condemned. It was a tense time to be a Bolton Wanderers fan, and the stakes couldn't have been too much higher when West Ham arrived at the Reebok.

The Hammers had been tagged by many in the media as a side that were 'Too Good to go Down', despite the fact that they had

On target: Henrik Pedersen scores against Chelsea in November.

started the season determined to disprove the theory. There was no question that West Ham were blessed with an amazingly talented crop of young home-grown players like Glen Johnson, Joe Cole, Michael Carrick and Jermain Defoe.

This golden quartet all promised a bright and potentially glorious future for the East End side. But their supporters also knew that relegation would almost inevitably lead to the break up of the team and the loss of their brightest lights.

And when they arrived at the Reebok there were only five games left in which to save their skins. Wanderers held an Okocha-inspired three-point advantage. The 27,000

plus who had packed into the Reebok knew that defeat for either side would have dreadful implications.

Okocha pulled on the white shirt more than 100 times during his four years at the Reebok, but if you were to ask him which was the most important his mind will flick right back to 19 April 2003. Not only was it his most important match, but it was probably his finest too because he never allowed the occasion or the fear factor to hinder his performance.

'The game against West Ham was probably one of my best for the club. We all knew how crucial it was. They were right behind us in the League, and it was between

Cole burns: Okocha sees off West Ham's Joe Cole, keeps his feet and takes aim...

us and them for the final relegation place. It is one of the most tense atmospheres I have ever played in.'

Fittingly, Okocha scored the only goal. But it wasn't the kind of scrambled effort that is so common in such tense encounters. Okocha's winner was a majestic bit of football from one of the world's great players. A goal

worthy of winning a Cup Final. In a sense it did. The relegation Cup Final.

It's a goal that is etched on Okocha's memory, and several years later he can still picture the scene clearly.

'When I picked the ball up West Ham were on the attack and I was in my own half. I looked up and I realised that I had some room in front of me so I decided to attack the space. As I ran into the West Ham half Joe Cole came to try to tackle me.'

This was the key moment. The fine line between glory and obscurity. As Cole slid in Okocha looked for a second as though he was about to come crashing to the earth. For a heart-stopping moment he stumbled but somehow he kept his feet, rode the tackle and retained possession.

'When I got past I looked up and realised that I was within shooting range. I thought "Why not take a shot?" and luckily for me I hit it well and it went in. For me that goal will always be number one on my list of the goals I scored during my time at Bolton because it came in such a high-pressure game.'

The shot from outside the box was a cracker. David James, one of the best goalkeepers of his generation, strained every sinew but to no avail, and a split second later the net was bulging. The Reebok reaction was joyous. Grown men who should know better were hugging complete strangers. The restraint and decorum that's brought about by all-seater stadiums was momentarily forgotten as joyous celebrations erupted with an intensity that has rarely been matched since that day.

Tense times: tempers boil over as the final whistle goes, with Bolton having beaten relegation rivals West Ham 1–0.

Job done. Well not quite. Okocha's brilliance came six minutes before half-time, which raised the small problem of hanging on for 51 minutes and stoppage time against a side who were fighting for their lives. Defoe missed a sitter, while Cole and Ian Pearce lost their heads before the final whistle, which was greeted with a Reebok roar that would have made the makers of Strepsils supremely happy.

Okocha had produced a world-class moment just when the club needed it most.

'I think that day ultimately did a lot of damage to West Ham's confidence and their hopes of staying up were given a huge blow,' says the Nigerian. 'It would certainly have been a massive blow to our confidence if the result had gone the other way.'

To their credit, West Ham refused to give up the fight and in the next round of matches they reduced the gap. As Wanderers were being held 0–0 at Blackburn Rovers, the Hammers managed a 1–0 win over Middlesbrough, despite the fact that their manager Glenn Roeder collapsed from a suspected brain haemorrhage.

So it was nail-biting time all over again.

Wanderers' next visitors to the Reebok were Arsenal. At that stage Arsene Wenger's men were going head to head against Manchester United in pursuit of the League title. Victory that day would have given the Gunners top spot.

With 56 minutes of the game gone, that result looked a mere formality. Sylvain Wiltord and Robert Pires looked to have put the game to bed with goals early in the second half. If that is how it had stayed this match wouldn't have merited so much of a footnote. However, it became a Reebok classic. Wanderers refused to give in. And for once in this roller-coaster relegation scrap it wasn't Okocha who earned the headlines.

Fittingly for a game against such a Gallic-influenced outfit, it was Wanderers' very own French World Cup-winning genius Youri Djorkaeff who inspired the comeback. Djorkaeff had a silky first touch and a wonderful eye for a pass, but he also possessed supreme battling qualities – qualities that were very much to the fore that day.

So when Seaman spilled a Per Frandsen piledriver Youri was first to react to knock home the rebound. What minutes earlier had seemed liked a hopeless cause was there for

Own up: Arsenal's Martin Keown scores an own-goal, and Bolton players celebrate an unlikely comeback.

the rescuing, and Martin Keown duly obliged by heading a well-flighted Djorkaeff free-kick into the top corner of his own net, 2–2. Cue more Reebok delirium. Wenger's expression on the touchline was a picture.

It was every bit as impressive as the fightback against Leicester the previous season had been. It even had Manchester United fans singing our praises.

West Ham, however, still refused to throw in the towel. Inspired by having their legendary ex-player Trevor Brooking in the dugout in place of Roeder, they kept on winning.

On 3 May 2003, the penultimate day of a draining campaign, Wanderers endured one of their toughest tests of character.

West Ham played earlier in the day and made it three wins out of three with a 1–0 victory over Chelsea. The three points were hugely significant as they took West Ham above Bolton who, thanks to TV schedules, were playing at 5.15pm at Southampton. Defeat for Wanderers would have put West Ham in pole position to avoid the drop.

'When the news came through that West Ham had won 1–0 it meant that we had to get at least a draw to go into the final game of the season with our destiny in our own hands,' says Allardyce. 'But for the players it felt as though they had played two games in one day, because everybody was so nervous and uptight about the result at West Ham. When it came through it was a real negative for them. Mentally it killed them. Quite how we got a 0–0 after that I don't know.

'I was watching from the dugout and world-class players like Okocha and Djorkaeff were suffering from fear. I hadn't seen that from them before. Jay Jay couldn't kick a ball. It was unbelievable how fear took over.

'I don't think we should have been asked to go through that by the TV people. I wouldn't let it happen again.'

The result at St Mary's meant that only goal difference separated Bolton from West Ham with one game to go. The final day of the season was played on Sunday 11 May. Wanderers prepared to take on Middlesbrough at the Reebok, while West Ham were travelling to Birmingham City. The build up was sickeningly tense.

'It was probably one of the worse weeks I've experienced in football,' says Allardyce.

'It was difficult to know what to do with the players. We concentrated on trying to keep the lads calm. We didn't want them getting too uptight, too agitated, and we didn't want them to expend too much nervous energy so relaxation was the big thing on the agenda. We decided to keep the training sessions as light and enjoyable as possible. Our focus was on trying to take pressure off the players and at the same time not giving them too much time to worry about the game against Middlesbrough.'

The equation was straightforward. Wanderers could guarantee their safety with a win. West Ham had to get a result better than Bolton's.

And thankfully Bolton had the artful Okocha.

Mid-table Middlesbrough arrived with very little to play for other than party-pooper status. Though to add spice to the occasion they had a striker in their ranks – a certain Michael Ricketts who had something of a point to prove following a January move from the Reebok. Maybe it helped that Ricketts, who at that point had failed to impress at Middlesbrough, had to settle for a place on the bench.

What Bolton really needed to settle the nerves was an early goal, and Per Frandsen

Seconds away: Jay Jay Okocha's twice taken free-kick flies into the Middlesbrough net to put Bolton 2–0 up on the final day of the season.

Relief: the Bolton management team and backroom staff celebrate as the final whistle means the club are safe from the drop.

Dread: anxious Bolton fans can hardly watch the action unfold on the final day.

duly obliged with a 20-yarder that fizzed past Mark Schwarzer after just 10 minutes.

In the previous weeks Okocha had been the catalyst. The man had kick-started the side when the frantic search for precious points seemed hopeless. His job against Middlesbrough was more poetic. His task was to get the party started.

Naturally he obliged. Wearing a T-shirt emblazoned 'Thank You Jesus' under his official club kit, he curled a delicious free-kick into the top corner of Schwarzer's goal with 21 minutes played. Wanderers were 2–0 up and no one cared what was happening at Birmingham. All the same it was wonderful to hear that West Ham were one down. Thank You Jesus indeed.

'We had a piece of good fortune with Jay Jay's free-kick,' says Allardyce. 'The referee made him take it twice. He had missed with the first one, but of course he scored when he took it a second time. It's those sorts of things that make a difference between staying up and going down.'

The tension that had been building for nine months was dispelled. The noose had been slipped and the champagne corks could be popped. But wait, the season had

Jubilation: the final whistle is greeted with scenes of joy on the Reebok terraces.

been too dramatic not to provide one final twist.

Ricketts, a half-time substitute, scored his first goal for Middlesbrough with an hour gone.

'It had to be against us!' says Allardyce. 'When that goal went in I started wondering whether they would get an equaliser. Naturally, we were following events at Birmingham too, and a few minutes after Ricketts's goal at the Reebok West Ham scored.'

It meant Wanderers were just a Middlesbrough leveller away from relegation. A relegation that would, in all likelihood, have meant the end of the Reebok road for many of the stars of that side like N'Gotty, Djorkaeff and Okocha at a time when the club was trying to build rather than dismantle.

The game's final moments were a fitting reflection of the weeks that had preceded. They were played out in a stomach-churning mix of anxiety, fear, hope and finally elation.

Bolton managed to hang on so that referee Rob Styles's final whistle sparked a huge Reebok party.

With music pounding from the PA, the players performed a deserved lap of honour around an emotionally-drained Reebok.

There's an oft-repeated TV clip of Allardyce attempting the Okocha shuffle during the celebrations.

Okocha looks back on that time with great fondness. 'The Reebok will always be special to me. The people and the club were all so friendly. It was like being part of one extended family, and I will never forget it.'

In a team sport it is difficult to credit one man with the results of an entire season. And certainly Okocha would be the last to make such a bold claim. But in reflecting on Bolton Wanderers' 2002–03 campaign it is hard to overstate Jay Jay's influence on the eventual outcome.

As world-class players have always done, Okocha dazzled even when the tension was at its peak.

Top 10 Jay Jay moments

1. Second goal against Aston Villa 5–2, 21 January 2004
2. Decision to stay for semi-final (see 1), 20 January 2004
3. Twice taken life-saving free kick against Middlesbrough 2–1, 11 May 2003
4. Flicking the ball over Ray Parlour's head in a tight corner against Arsenal, 26 April 2003
5. Spat with Tal Ben Haim against West Ham, 11 March 2006
6. Winning goal against West Ham, 11 April 2003
7. Opening goal of the season against Charlton, 14 August 2004
8. Hitting the bar three times against Tottenham 1–0 at White Hart Lane, 1 November 2003
9. The dancing goal celebration against Tottenham 1–0, 24 March 2003
10. Jay Jay arrives with a thundering strike against Newcastle, Boxing Day 2002

2002–03

Ins

Pierre Yves-Andre (loan, FC Nantes), Chris Armstrong (Tottenham Hotspur), Akin Bulent (loan, Galatasaray), Ivan Campo (Real Madrid), Delroy Facey (Huddersfield Town), David Holdsworth (Birmingham City), Florent Laville (loan, Lyon), Bernard Mendy (loan, Paris Saint-Germain), Jay Jay Okocha (Paris Saint-Germain), Salva Ballesta (loan, Valencia), Jonathan Walters (Blackburn Rovers), Cleveland Taylor (trainee).

Outs

Gudni Bergsson (Retired), Salva Ballesta (loan, Valencia), Bernard Mendy (loan, Paris Saint-Germain), Pierre Yves-Andre (loan, FC Nantes), Chris Armstrong (Wrexham), Colin Hendry (retired), Dean Holdsworth (Coventry City), David Holdsworth (Scarborough), David Norris (Plymouth Argyle), Michael Ricketts (Middlesbrough), Nicky Southall (Gillingham), Rod Wallace (Gillingham), Steve Banks (Stoke City), Salva Ballesta (loan, Valencia), Akin Bulent (loan, Galatasaray), Pierre Yves-Andre (loan, FC Nantes).

Chapter Seven

All You Need Is Love

'My lowest point came during a training session. The first team was playing against the reserve team. I wasn't even selected for the reserves. I was left on the sidelines, just watching. I rang my agent and told him "Get me out of here – just get me out of here!"'

Football clubs can be very unforgiving places when your face doesn't fit. Players can be the poster pin-up one day and spurned by fans and coaches the next. There are times when you know you are better off moving. For Kevin Davies the time was Spring 2003, the place Southampton. The then Saints boss Gordon Strachan wasn't a big fan of the striker, or if he was he had a funny way of letting Davies know. No matter what he did, Strachan didn't seem to notice.

'The last year at Southampton was a particularly tricky one for me,' says Davies. 'I had been through a few ups and downs in my career before. Even so, that stage of my career was very tough. Basically the manager gave me the cold shoulder. I felt I should have been in the team a little bit more, but the manager didn't. I would try really hard in training, that didn't work. I scored goals in the reserves, that didn't work. Whatever I did wasn't enough. In the end I felt it was personal. I went out on loan [to Millwall] to try and play some games, so at least other managers could see me. By that time I hadn't played a lot, so I was a little bit out of shape.'

Saint Kevin: striker Kevin Davies returns to Southampton and scores for Bolton.

Short of match fitness and not exactly brimming over with confidence, Davies hardly did himself justice. Rock bottom was reached when he was completely neglected for the firsts v reserves training match. That season, Southampton made it through to the FA Cup Final. But even that memory is a bitter one for Davies. 'I wasn't selected and after the Final the manager told me that was it.'

Five years earlier Davies had been signed by Blackburn Rovers for £7.5 million and was being touted as a future England international. Illness, injury and an unhappy dressing room meant that Ewood Park was a grim place for the Sheffield-born striker, and in 2000 he returned to Southampton. But by the summer of 2003 the 26-year-old found himself at a major crossroads – he was clubless and his reputation was in desperate need of reviving.

He found redemption at Bolton Wanderers – the right club at the right time. There was a spin-off from the club's policy to bring in Bosman 'frees' and loan players. By taking players that weren't wanted or appreciated at their former clubs and lavishing them with the kind of care and attention a 17-year-old might on his first car, Wanderers gained a reputation for reviving careers.

Not only that, they offered players a chance to play in the Premier League. Prior to Youri Djorkaeff's arrival at the Reebok in 2002, he had been banished to the Kaiserslautern youth team for six months. At the start of the following season, Ivan Campo and Jay Jay Okocha followed him through the doors. Campo had not been given a squad number at Real Madrid, while Jay Jay had suffered an indifferent experience towards the end of his spell at Paris Saint-Germain. At Bolton, they were allowed to flourish again. All it took was a bit of nurturing, a bit of love, a bit of caring. It was fundamental to the spirit of the club. All the new faces quickly became part of the Bolton Wanderers family. The environment, the personal touch, the intimacy, were all the cornerstones of the club. This was the Wanderers brand. This was the club that in the summer of 2003 offered a home to Kevin Davies.

On arrival at Bolton he was put on trial – a situation some may have balked, given he'd been in the Premier League for the past seven years. But Davies accepted that his fall from grace as a Saint had left question marks about him.

'I was out of contract and had to prove myself when I came to Bolton,' says Davies. 'I was invited by the club to Bormio in Italy during the pre-season fitness work out and then on to Ireland, where I played a couple of games and everything went okay. I never viewed it as a step down or felt offended about having to prove myself, because at the time I could have been looking at a move to a Championship side. Bolton were offering me the chance to continue to play in the Premier League, which was great as far as I was concerned. I always felt I could play at this level, and I was delighted to be handed another chance. It helped that what I discovered here was a great working environment, because I'd obviously just been through a bad time at Southampton and prior to that at Blackburn, where the dressing room wasn't great.'

In Italy and then in Ireland, Davies worked hard on his fitness and in the warm-up games did enough to impress Allardyce and his coaching team that he was worth taking a chance on. He was offered a one-year contract with the possibility of an extension.

'As soon as Bolton offered me something, there was no hesitation. I was delighted to sign.'

'The staff here looked after me and started working with me to get me into decent shape, and they have been working with me ever since. We have such a good backroom staff – there's 20 or so of them and they are all here to help players in various ways. I know how difficult it can be going to a new club and trying to settle in. It must be even more difficult if you are in a foreign country and the language is different. But here at Bolton there is a tremendous group of people who can help you in all sorts of ways – if you want to find a house, sort out paying bills and so on. It isn't a surprise to me that most players who come here settle in really well. They are made to feel part of the club straight away. It is important for the club that you are made to feel comfortable, because the whole squad spends an awful lot of time together. For 10 months we are together, day in and day out. The club is like a second family and it is crucial that it is a happy family.'

One of the key members of that support team is Matt Hockin. He originally joined the backroom staff from Manchester City as a video analyst, which brought him into constant contact with the players and coaches. After a while he hit on the idea that a player liaison role would interest him and help ensure the players felt at home as speedily as possible.

He works alongside Sue Whittle and together they try to make sure the transition to life at the Reebok is straightforward for new players and that existing ones only have to concentrate on their football.

'When players come here they very often don't know much about the place and don't know where they'll be living,' says Matt. 'Everything is very new to them. So Sue and I help them in lots of practical ways. We help them get cars, find houses, schools for their children and that sort of thing. Obviously, for some of the foreign players it is a new country and new culture, and they need all sorts of help, but I also look after the British players who are simply new to the club. The role day to day is very reactionary. There are lots of trips to airports, lots of phone calls. One of the most important parts of the job is the fact that the players know that there's someone on the end of a phone for them. There is a point when you can suffocate a player by doing too much and there comes a point where you have to guide them. That said, a lot of players are very organised anyway.'

Matt is one of the first faces players see when they arrive at the club. 'When someone comes to sign or for a trial, it tends to be me who meets them at the airport. That's all part of the job. You can have a good relationship with them at that point. I try to keep it light, and they don't see me as a decision maker. It works very well. I also look after the staff quite a bit too. I love the job to be honest. I go to a lot of games, mix with the players and the staff, and for someone with a passion for football, what could be better? I never complain.'

With this sort of back-up, Davies was instantly embraced by the Bolton family, though the period of relative inactivity at Southampton had taken its toll physically.

'Strength and conditioning coach Mark Howard has worked with me from day one. When I first came I needed to lose a bit of weight, and I was a bit out of condition. Mark and the team worked really hard with me and continue to today. [At the start of the 2006–07 season, Davies was 12 kilos lighter than when he'd first arrived at the club.] Each year I try to get fitter and fitter. Different players might need different types of training, whether it is speed or strength, and everyone has a tailor-made programme for them.

Masked attacker: Bolton's Youri Djorkaeff, who started the 2003–04 season wearing a protective mask because of an injury collected in pre-season.

Bolton has always been at the forefront when there have been any new advances in techniques. Every aspect is geared to trying to help us find that extra percentage throughout the season. Every angle is looked at. I have been at a few other clubs in my career and nowhere I know is as far advanced as this.

'When we train we wear heart rate monitors each day to see how hard we are pushing ourselves. The coaches use the data to check whether we are training too hard or not hard enough. You are assessed each and every day and the information is then used to

decide the type of training to do. The players have faith in what we are doing because it has been shown to work.'

Davies wasn't the only new face on the training ground that summer. Stelios Giannakopoulos was signed for £1 million from Olympiakos, where he'd won a truck load of medals. In contrast, Ibrahim Ba came from AC Milan with a reputation to repair.

But the summer signing that really grabbed the headlines was that of Mario Jardel from Sporting Lisbon. Jardel's playing record, and more specifically his goals record at Porto, Galatasaray and Sporting, was incredible. In one season with Sporting he'd scored 42 goals in 30 games! In Portuguese football he scored 150 goals in 146 games, but his life became dogged with personal issues that spilled over to his professional career. And first sightings of the striker in Bolton suggested those issues were still dogging him. Jardel was completely out of shape.

Despite the excess pounds, his CV was enough to convince Allardyce that it was worth taking a gamble on the Brazilian and trying to rehabilitate his career.

Stelios and Davies were the only ones to feature on the opening day of the season, but neither will want to be reminded of their Bolton debut, which ended in a 4–0 drubbing against Manchester United at Old Trafford. The season had got off to a grim start and it was to get worse. Davies scored against his old club Blackburn Rovers on his home debut, but Wanderers allowed a 2–0 lead to slip as Dwight Yorke poached an injury-time equaliser. Then a Teddy Sheringham hat-trick condemned the side to a 4–0 defeat at Fratton Park.

Rover-joyed: Youri Djorkaeff and Henrik Pedersen celebrate after the Frenchman gives Bolton the lead against Blackburn Rovers at the Reebok.

On target: Davies scores in a 1–1 draw against Wolves.

win of the season, beating Middlesbrough 2–0 with Davies once more on the score sheet.

Jardel, 10 kilos lighter than when he'd originally paraded before the press in August, finally made his first start for the club in late September. Despite looking some way off the pace, he managed to score twice as Wanderers eased past Walsall in the Carling Cup.

In the Premier League, however, it was Wanderers who were the lightweights as their stuttering start continued. After 10 games

Brazilian defender Emerson Thome was signed ahead of the transfer deadline from Sunderland. He helped shore up the leaky backline, and Wanderers picked up their first

Super Mario: summer signing Mario Jardel celebrates a goal in the League Cup tie against Walsall.

Cup heroes: Youri Djorkaeff and Jay Jay Okocha give Bolton a stunning League Cup victory at Liverpool.

they still only had one win to their name and another relegation scrap looked likely. The Carling Cup was a welcome respite. A comfortable 2–0 win over Gillingham kept Wanderers interested and sparked an improved run in the League with Wanderers going through November unbeaten.

The Carling Cup had reached the quarter-final stage, but Wanderers faced a daunting trip to Liverpool. In the previous two seasons Allardyce had taken a great deal of flak for his policy of playing weakened sides in the Cup competitions, but he was unrepentant.

'The Premier League was still the most important thing, and we were still a good way off being safe at that particular time of year.

'Before the Liverpool Cup match I had to make some tough decisions about who to play and who to rest. The Christmas period was coming up, and we had stats that showed that when we played two games in a week we tended to struggle because our squad was the oldest in the Premier League at that time. That meant we had to maximise it as best we could.'

Maximising the squad meant rotation. Allardyce made seven changes to the team that had just beaten Everton in the League. Jardel made another start and Djorkaeff returned from a long injury lay-off.

The two combined to give Wanderers the perfect start, with Jardel heading home a Djorkaeff corner after just three minutes. Danny Murphy levelled in the second half, before Okocha scored with a magnificent free-kick to restore Bolton's advantage in the 79th minute. Valadimir Smicer equalised again for Liverpool with a thumping long-range effort two minutes from time. Then in injury time Davies was hacked down in the box and Djorkaeff held his nerve to fire home from the penalty spot.

That game was to be Jardel's last significant moment in a Bolton shirt. After failing to impress he left for Ancona in Italy in January.

While his move to Bolton hadn't worked, it was a different story for Davies. Already he had become a vital member of the Wanderers first-team squad. He wasn't prolific but his physical presence, alongside the sublime skills of Djorkaeff and Okocha, was proving to be an effective weapon in Wanderers' armoury. Davies was also an instant hit with the Reebok supporters, thanks to his lung-

busting displays. His work rate, desire and his ability to intimidate defenders when they were in possession helped make Wanderers a tough side to play against.

'The season was a massive turnaround for me personally,' says Davies. 'It is something I worked really hard to make happen and, of course, the club helped me as well.'

The Carling Cup semi-final against David O'Leary's Aston Villa was to be played over two legs in January. And, thanks to improved results in the Premier League, Wanderers were able to approach the game from the relative comfort of mid-table.

A remarkable 4–3 win at Ewood Park against Blackburn Rovers had been followed up with a more regulation 1–0 victory over

Kevin Heaven: Nolan and Davies savour victory over Spurs at White Hart Lane.

Portsmouth. The latter was marked by a tireless man-of-the-match display from the reinvigorated Davies, who scored the only goal.

Those points were priceless for Allardyce because they meant that for the first time in several seasons he could afford to play his strongest hand in a Cup tie – dispensing with his usual rotation policy.

Just how strong a side he would have at his disposal was the subject of fierce pre-match debate. Three thousand miles away, the African Nations Cup was about to get under way, and Jay Jay Okocha was expected to report for duty for Nigeria – before the first leg.

'We did everything we could to make sure we got Jay Jay to stay for the game. Jay Jay is the David Beckham of Nigeria and everybody absolutely adores the man there. So we asked him to use that power and influence to see if he could turn up a little bit later than originally planned for the African Nations Cup,' says Allardyce.

Okocha was torn. He didn't want to let his club or his country down. 'The gaffer asked me to delay my flight until after the semi-final, saying it would give the team a good send off. It put me in trouble with the national coach, but as things turned out I am glad I did it, because looking back it was a game worth waiting for.'

It took just two minutes for Okocha to vindicate Allardyce's judgement. The Nigerian scored direct from a free-kick that completely wrong-footed Villa 'keeper Thomas Sorensen. All smiles, Jay Jay ran to the touchline beaming at the manager.

It got better. Kevin Nolan made it 2–0 after nine minutes with a low drive from the edge of the box. Then on 17 minutes Stelios put Wanderers 3–0 in front with a scissor kick from a Davies flick-on. The Reebok was alive and Wanderers had one foot in the Cardiff Final, or so it seemed. Villa hit back, and Angel pulled a goal back with a cross-cum-shot after 20 minutes. When he grabbed a second after the break to make it 3–2 it set the nerves jangling. But on this special night Bolton weren't going to be denied. Their two-goal cushion was restored, first by a thumping Bruno N'Gotty header from a Djorkaeff corner, but the goal of the game was still to come.

With time ticking away, Wanderers won a free-kick on the left edge of the Villa penalty area. The visitors assembled a two-man wall

Semi-sation: Jay Jay Okocha's free-kick puts Wanderers on course for a memorable victory in the first leg of the League Cup semi final against Aston Villa.

and, given the angle, Okocha's only sensible option appeared to be to cross. The thought never entered his head. He sprinted up to the ball and smacked it with the outside of his foot to send it spearing into the top corner of the stunned Sorensen's goal.

Okocha reckons it's one of his best in a Bolton shirt, and it is difficult to argue with him. 'I always believe that when it comes to shooting, if you don't buy a ticket you won't win the lottery. You have to have a go. When we got the free-kick I knew I would have to go for power rather than accuracy because of the angle – it was the only way I would be able to beat a top-class goalkeeper. I struck it really well and it went in before he could react properly.'

It capped a breathless 5–2 Bolton victory. For once the hyperbole that surrounds the sport was thoroughly justified during the post-match analysis. Okocha was hailed by Allardyce as 'the best player the club had ever had'.

Even now Allardyce can't stop himself getting excited by the memory of that night. 'On a day when it really mattered, Jay Jay delivered. The goal he scored from the free-kick, when he bent it round the wall with the outside of his foot, was one to be remembered for a long, long time. In the process he had given us a great opportunity to get through to a major Cup Final.

'The whole of the 90 minutes was one of the best games I've ever been a part of –

either as a player or a manager – and it is without a doubt one of the best I have seen at the Reebok. It had everything: excitement, drama and goals – lots of goals, lots of high-quality goals.'

The Aston Villa game also underscored Allardyce's philosophy of trying to bring in talents like Okocha and Djorkaeff.

'Jay Jay was tremendous that night. That's why he's world class. And that's why you need world-class players – to make the difference. Both Jay Jay and Youri were world-class players. They both scored goals when you needed it most. Sometimes you might have heard people say "He didn't do much in that game." But in his first season with us at Charlton Youri scored two goals that were absolutely vital.

'Then, the following season at Charlton, we were playing some dreadful football, when out of the blue a ball dropped on Youri's chest, and he produced an overhead-kick into the top corner – a world-class goal and an important goal, because it won us the game. All his goals were important. All his goals were crucial.

'Jay Jay's were too. When we needed him most he would come up with the goods. In between, he probably didn't do an awful lot, but he would just produce those few seconds of magic and create something out of nothing. That's what those kind of players can do. They always tip the balance back in your favour, so that if you were losing they'd get you a draw, if you were drawing they'd get you a win. That's the difference between being in the top half and the bottom half.'

On the morning after the Villa game, Okocha jetted off to Africa. Job done. For his teammates, there was still the small matter of the second leg at Villa Park to come. Although 5–2 up, Wanderers would have to negotiate the tie without their inspirational talisman.

'Jay Jay had given us a comfortable cushion, but without it I don't think we'd have got through,' says Allardyce.

A week later, in the second leg at Villa Park, Thomas Hitzlsperger gave the hosts hope with an early goal, but when Gavin McCann was sent off for a foul on Jaaskelainen before half-time Wanderers appeared to be in total command. However, Villa increased their lead on the night through Jlloyd Samuel with a couple of minutes to go. That goal made the aggregate scores 5–4, and Villa only needed another to take the tie on the away-goals rule. It therefore set up a very nervy finale. Thankfully, Wanderers managed to hold on to book their place in the Final.

'Even with Aston Villa going down to 10 men quite early on, there was still an awful lot of tension and apprehension,' remembers Allardyce. 'We were trying to win through to a major Final for the first time for a while, and it was difficult. But we had done enough in the first leg at the Reebok to earn our place.'

Having suffered the heartache of missing out on a place in the Southampton FA Cup Final squad the previous May, Davies was determined to make this Final. 'It became a little bit edgy towards the end. Anthony Barness made a last-ditch clearance with a few minutes to go to keep us in the game, and when the final whistle went there was a mixture of relief and delight for us. I remember going back to the hotel that night and we had a little celebration planned. We were having the odd glass of champagne,

Carling time: Bolton players celebrate in the Villa Park dressing room after securing their place in the League Cup Final.

Lots of bottle: Big Sam takes time to drink in Bolton's achievement – reaching a major Cup Final.

when I got a call from my partner to say she was going into labour – so I had to get a taxi back to Bolton pretty quickly. It was a pretty memorable night all round!

'That night represented a big turnaround both on and off the pitch for me. When I was at Southampton I was young and single, and it was a difficult time for me because of how things were with the manager there. Now, a few months later, I had settled down, had a young family and was playing football regularly. Everything on the pitch and off the pitch was just perfect for me.'

Sunday 29 February 2004 and Wanderers were back at the Millennium Stadium, Cardiff. Steve McClaren's Middlesbrough stood in the way of Bolton and their first major trophy for almost 50 years. Middlesbrough, who had won their semi-final against Arsenal, were looking for the first piece of silverware in their history. The Teesside club's chairman, Steve Gibson, had invested millions to get to this stage.

And for both clubs there was an added carrot – a place in the UEFA Cup awaited the winners. Wanderers, who had spent the last

Here wig go: Bolton fans in party mood in Cardiff ahead of the Carling Cup Final.

Final time: Kevin Davies steps out at Cardiff as Bolton prepare to take on Middlesbrough.

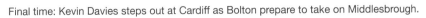

two seasons frantically trying to avoid relegation, were suddenly one game away from Europe.

It was an incredible incentive – though winning the trophy was the only concern for the players.

'Walking out of the tunnel at Cardiff was one of those special moments for me,' says Davies. 'These are memories that you take with you from the game. The things that make it special.'

Davies can even look back on a Cup Final with fond memories of a goal. Unfortunately, his strike was only a consolation. The Cup

went to McClaren's men after Joseph-Desire Job and Bolo Zenden had put Middlesbrough 2–0 up inside seven minutes. Davies made it 2–1 in the 21st minute, but that's how it finished. Losing a Final is never a nice feeling, but the dejection felt by players and supporters was compounded by the notion that Wanderers didn't do themselves full justice. Okocha couldn't rediscover his semi-final brilliance and Youri Djorkaeff failed to take the chances that came his way.

It was probably the one major occasion when Wanderers' star players failed to deliver on the big stage.

Blimey oh Riley: Jay Jay Okocha appeals in vain to referee Mike Riley after Middlesbrough are awarded an early penalty.

Down and out: Okocha and Emerson Thome sink to the turf at the final whistle.

'Unfortunately we lost it in the first 10 minutes of the Final,' says Allardyce, who in his post-match interviews turned his attentions to referee Mike Riley – the man who'd been in charge of the infamous Leicester game at the Reebok a couple of seasons earlier.

'We've always had a problem with Mike Riley in our recent history,' raged Allardyce. 'He hasn't been kind to us, to say the least. And, unfortunately, I have to say he lived up to his reputation as far as we are concerned. Our fans showed their disapproval by booing him when he went up for his medal.'

There were two particular incidents which infuriated the Bolton manager – both concerning penalties. The first was Zenden's spot-kick. The Dutchman fell as he took it and kicked the ball twice, which in the Bolton boss's view had wrong-footed Jussi Jaaskelainen. His second charge was that Wanderers should have had a penalty of their own in the 89th minute when Ugo Ehiogu handled a Stelios shot.

Despite the disappointment, actually getting to the Final was a turning point. The club had come within 90 minutes of Europe. Qualification for European football had become a realistic possibility. And it was to Europe they started to turn their attentions in the weeks and months ahead.

Inevitably there was something of a hangover from the Millennium Stadium defeat. When Wanderers returned from South Wales and resumed their League campaign they suffered three successive defeats. Thankfully, the rot was eventually stopped by an audacious Henrik Pedersen winner against Newcastle, when the Dane hit a shot from an acute angle that somehow looped over Shay Given.

With eight games to go, Wanderers were virtually safe from relegation. Now they started to shift a gear. They reeled off five successive wins – unheard of in the club's Premier League days, including a 4–1 defeat of Leeds United. That result all but confirmed the relegation of the Yorkshire giants, who only a couple of seasons earlier had been playing in the semi-finals of the Champions League.

For the millions watching on television, Leeds's amazing fall from grace was graphically etched on the tearful face on one young United supporter at the Reebok that day. When their relegation was picked over by

the pundits, much was made about the money the Elland Road club had invested in players because Leeds were now facing financial ruin. It contrasted sharply with the practices adopted by the Bolton board and their policy of hunting for bargains in the summer sales.

As the season came to a climax, Wanderers were linked with a dramatic swoop for the legendary Brazilian forward Rivaldo. He was one of the most coveted stars in the world, who had left Barcelona a year earlier for AC Milan, but had endured a disappointing 12 months in Italy. The potential deal had supporters savouring the mouth-watering prospect of watching a future Bolton side line up with Jay Jay Okocha, Youri Djorkaeff and Rivaldo in their ranks.

It looked like a perfect Wanderers deal. Rivaldo was 32, so still had something to offer. And Allardyce had pulled off similar coups in the past, so why not this one? Sadly, after an on-off saga which lasted well into the close season, the player eventually decided to go to Greek side Olympiakos.

In the meantime, Wanderers' charge up the table continued at a pace. Post Cardiff, Djorkaeff was back to his sublime best. He scored twice to earn Bolton a 2–1 win at Everton in the penultimate game of the campaign. The result lifted the club to seventh in the table and took the points tally to 56 – a club record in the Premier League. Not only that, it guaranteed Bolton their best finish in the top flight of English football for 44 years.

Their final game of the season at home to Fulham brought an end to the winning streak, the Londoners securing a 2–0 victory. The defeat couldn't dampen the buoyant mood within the Reebok. The club had finished in eighth place in the table and runners-up in one of the major Cup competitions. After three seasons back in the Premier League, Bolton Wanderers had arrived.

Three successive seasons in the top flight, combined with the growing influence of Eddie Davies behind the scenes, meant that the club's financial status was changing too.

The club still carried debts but, says chief executive Allan Duckworth, the banks had much more confidence in the business operation. 'In some respects the size of the debt isn't that important really,' he says. 'The important thing is your ability to service it. You have to be able to pay the interest off and,

in most cases, banks still want you to pay some of the capital off as you go on as well. Then the banks look at the security you have in case anything goes wrong. In the early years we weren't making enough money to service the debt. But since then Eddie Davies put in more capital, and he has stood behind the company as a guarantor. Basically he said he would guarantee the club if anything goes wrong. We no longer had the sword of Damocles hanging over us all the time.'

It was the perfect stable environment that allowed Kevin Davies to settle in. The player who, as much as Djorkaeff and Okocha, epitomised the club's recruitment methods had found a new home.

'I have always thought that the Reebok is a special place to play football,' he says. 'I pass the place every day going to training and it is such a landmark off the M61. Over the years it has become a difficult place for teams to visit, and it has become a good place for us to play and we all enjoy playing there. Friends who come up from down south love the stadium. It stands out and the kids always notice it. It's a great place to play.'

Davies had recovered from his humiliation at Southampton thanks to a bit of care and attention from the Bolton backroom staff. At the Reebok, he felt wanted and on the pitch he had a role that played to his strengths; more than that he was loved, particularly by the fans.

And, despite being surrounded by the likes of world-class talents like Djorkaeff and Okocha, it was Davies who ran away with the end-of-season Player of the Year award. His energetic displays had made him a real crowd favourite.

A decade earlier another striker, John McGinlay, had been the terrace hero. McGinlay was revered not only for his goals but for the wholehearted determination he showed every time he pulled on a Bolton shirt. In Davies they had a modern day successor, a player every bit as combative and dedicated.

His story showed that anything was possible. You simply had to take your chances and believe. It was an ethos that was about to be adopted by the club as a whole as they set their sights on the big prize: Europe.

Best 10 Goals at the Reebok Stadium

Jay Jay Okocha against Aston Villa (second goal)
Nicolas Anelka against Arsenal
Les Ferdinand against Manchester United
Eidur Gudjohnsen against Wimbledon
Jay Jay Okocha against West Ham United
Ricardo Gardner against Newcastle United
Gudni Bergsson against Barnsley
Jimmy Phillips against Crystal Palace
Per Frandsen against Middlesbrough
Henrik Pedersen against Newcastle United

2003–04

Ins
Ibrahim Ba (AC Milan), Stelios (Olympiakos), Steve Howey (Leicester City), Mario Jardel (Sporting Lisbon), Javi Moreno (loan, Atletico Madrid), Glen Little (loan, Burnley), Jon Otsemobor (loan, Liverpool), Dwight Pezzarossi (Racing de Ferrol), Donovan Ricketts (Village United), Emerson Thome (Sunderland), Ricardo Vaz Te (trainee), Kevin Davies (Southampton), Charlie Comyn-Platt (trainee).

Outs
Delroy Facey (West Bromwich Albion), Steve Howey (New England Revolution), Mario Jardel (Newell's Old Boys), Jermaine Johnson (Oldham Athletic), Jon Otsemobor (loan, Liverpool), Dwight Pezzarossi (Comunicaciones), Leam Richardson (Blackpool), Jeff Smith (Preston North End), Cleveland Taylor (Scunthorpe United), Jonathan Walters (Hull City). Paul Warhurst (Chesterfield), Mike Whitlow (Sheffield United), Javi Moreno (loan, Atletico Madrid), Glen Little (loan, Burnley).

The Euro Visionaries

It's important at this stage to put things in perspective. Following a very brief couple of seasons in Division One in the late 1970s, Wanderers had spent most of the 1980s in what appeared to be terminal decline. The low point was reached at the end of the 1986–87 season when the club was relegated to Division Four for the first time in its history.

Set in those terms, the revival, initially sparked by Bruce Rioch in the early 90s, has been nothing short of astonishing.

But how do you transform a football club?

How do you take a club that is struggling to keep its head above water financially, one that has rarely featured in the top flight for decades, one thats glory days are just distant

Masterplanners: Big Sam, chief scout Jack Chapman and psychologist Mike Forde compare notes during a pre-season game in the summer of 2004.

black and white memories, and then turn it into one that consistently challenges for European competition?

The answer: first believe you can, and then plan for it to happen.

Throughout Allardyce's reign, Wanderers had been paupers by the standards of the Premier League, but despite that the manager was given his head to engineer a Reebok revolution. The board realised that while they could not afford to compete in terms of transfer fees or at the very top end wages, backing Allardyce's innovative plans to develop the backroom staff and invest in an array of technology made financial sense.

Says Gartside, 'Right from the word go Sam was very passionate about developing the sport science side of the club. When Sam would come along and say "I want another physio" or whatever, my thinking was simple. I knew that if the new physio could help us get one player fitter one game earlier then it would be worth it. A player's wages for a couple of weeks would cover what the new guy would earn in a year. This had to make sense for the club. It's not just the cost of the people, it's about the facilities too. We have spent around £4 million on the training

ground and now have one of the best in the Premier League.'

One of the early arrivals in 1999 was sports psychologist Mike Forde. With hindsight, his appointment seems a masterstroke, though initially Forde met a degree of resistance from within the dressing room.

'When I came in I was only 24, straight out of university. I'd come back from America with loads of positive ideas,' he says. 'I walked into the club to find a set of lads who were going through a transition at the time. We had a solid group of players and some strong characters like Mike Whitlow, Colin Hendry and Ian Marshall, who were tough guys and who made a living playing in a tough era. It was a difficult time for me because I was trying to win over a group of people when there was a degree of natural scepticism around. One of the lines I remember hearing at the time was "this is only for weak players", which was something that you could either resist or say "well, okay, that's your perception".

'Every session I did in the early days, when I was trying to gain credibility, was important, and I always had the support of Sam and Phil [Brown], which was crucial at

A plus: Mike Forde explains some key principles during a training ground workshop.

that time. I was only a young guy, but they would always be there when the group got out of hand.'

It wasn't long, however, before the barriers were broken down and Forde had the allies he needed in the dressing room. Players like Gudni Bergsson, Per Frandsen and Dean Holdsworth quickly bought into what he was trying to do.

'They were strong characters, so when the lads started messing around a bit, they were the ones who would try and get the sessions back on track and keep things focused. That was all a learning experience for me.'

In those formative days, Forde established a working group of four players, which included Whitlow and Colin Hendry, and started putting a code of conduct in place. 'At first, we simply talked over a cup of tea about certain situations, case studies, that crop up and eventually put together a document which still stands as the players' code of conduct today – except now it's in three languages.'

But Forde took things a stage further.

'Instead of publishing a document which was simply a list of rules and regulations like in most businesses, I wanted to deliver something that was both practical and at the same time inspirational. We came up with something called *The Bolton Bible*. It was an A5 document and as well as the standard things like the team code of conduct, medical standards, sport science and so on, I put in chapters like What is an inspirational dream? What is the greatest imaginable challenge we could face? What are the attributes of a high performance team? It was all very glossy, leather bound, and it was very, very different for the sport. Each chapter had a video with it, like Lance Armstrong talking about his greatest victories and other classic stuff like that.'

After six months' work on *The Bolton Bible*, Forde decided it needed to be presented for the first time on a grand stage – so naturally he chose the Reebok.

'We wanted to give it a bit of an aura, which is why we chose the Reebok as the setting, and it was presented by the chairman Phil Gartside. It was a real landmark for the club because we were saying for the first time 'This is where we want Bolton Wanderers to go as a club. This is the manager's vision. This is where we are all heading. This phenomenal stadium that we walked into deserves a team that plays in the Premier League.'

'That was 12 months into my time at the club, but for me it was a watershed moment, because there were no longer any excuses around what we were aiming to do.'

What *The Bolton Bible* boiled down to was Forde sitting down with the rest of the staff, the players, the medics, the coaches and asking the simple question 'What do we want to achieve?' Many individuals had talked about the hopes and dreams of fans and players, but now Forde had distilled it into a mission statement for the club that every member could instantly understand and buy into.

Says Forde, 'We used to hold away days at Shaw Hill, and I remember during my second year at the club being at one and passing round a handout. It was quite a few years before we got into Europe, but on the front page I'd put a picture of the UEFA Cup.

'It was a way of profiling the next level, the inspirational dream, and Phil Brown was positive about it straight away, saying "Why can't we get there?" which was classic Phil. Sam and I were a little bit more reserved. I recall saying that strategically we've got to have certain things in place and wanting something is just not enough. You've got to have things, players, instruction time and resources in place to support you. We knew there had been cases of people getting into Europe and going down next year – like Ipswich Town – because they didn't have the resources to cope. Ipswich finished fifth one season and they even beat Inter Milan at home the year they went down. We couldn't forget that.

'You can never out-perform your "self concept". For example, if we said "Next season we're going to win the Premier League," it would be difficult to achieve as there are no frames of reference in the past – none. Looking around, is the stadium one that a Premier League winning team plays at? Yeah, course it is. But is the fan base big enough? The commercial sponsorship? The TV interest? The players wanting to play for us? All that would be a big, big sell. It'd take some hypnotism to pull that one off. But we could work out what the next level for the club was and, once we had finished eighth, the next level for us was to finish even higher and qualify for Europe.'

And by the start of the 2004–05 campaign, Forde's inspirational dream of UEFA Cup qualification was no longer just a photocopy on a sheet of paper. The other parts of the plan were falling into place. Thanks to Eddie Davies the club's finances were secure, Allardyce's backroom plans had progressed, and crucially he'd built a squad that had the ability to make it happen. And, in the shape of the Reebok, they had a stadium that lived up to the dream. Wanderers' self image had been transformed.

Clearly, European qualification didn't simply happen. It was a well-established aim long before it materialised. Every six weeks Forde took the staff away for a strategic-planning day, where they'd examine the next phase of the season and spend time brainstorming.

'We knew having a squad of quality players was vital too. I think getting the likes of Jay Jay Okocha, Bruno N'Gotty, Ivan Campo and Youri Djorkaeff in was important. Those players – and the fact that they wanted to play for us for whatever reason – was vital.

'Their own individual reasons for coming to Bolton didn't matter, but when you actually got close to them you thought "Hang on, I can influence this guy." Youri had won the World Cup, and yet he was listening to what we were saying and he was

Ready for action: the Wanderers dressing room at the Reebok.

implementing it. Ivan had won two European Cups with Real Madrid, and he was only 28 when he came here, and he too was still very motivated.

'I remember one of the members of staff said to us one day that if we got Ronaldo [the former Brazilian international] I think we could make an impact. It was not so much about getting him, it was the fact that we felt that confident – arrogant almost – that we could make a difference to such a great player. When we started to work with the likes of Bruno, Jay Jay, Youri and Ivan we got to thinking if we had 10 like them where could the team get to? Then all of a sudden your confidence, your self-image, your self-concept starts to grow.

'Another milestone in our development was getting into the Carling Cup Final the season before. The fact that we didn't win it was a disappointment, particularly considering who we were playing against. But we were within touching distance of Europe, so when the 2004–05 season started we were all clear that Europe was very much a possibility.

'The actual planning started two years beforehand. We had an away day for the staff at a hotel in Blackpool, and we put together a very clear and concise action plan. We worked out what we would need – the number of wins in a year, X number of clean sheets and so on. We knew exactly what we had to do and we started benchmarking our performance. We shared this with the players and, as a group, the staff had a very clear and concise plan.

'We knew that the year before 56 points had been enough to get into Europe, and we had finished eighth with 53 points. So at the start of that season we did a baseline plan of what qualification for Europe actually looks like. We knew, for example, that a good start was crucial.'

Wanderers players responded with a dazzling 4–1 opening-day victory over Charlton, with Jay Jay Okocha and Henrik Pedersen both scoring twice.

The make-up of the team was interesting, for the backroom boys had analysed data from previous seasons about how to get off to a winning start and realised that it was important to avoid selecting a team that included too many players with little or no previous Premier League experience. So Allardyce, having strengthened the squad with a number of new faces including Tal Ben

In with a shout: new signing Tal Ben Haim had to wait in the wings before making his mark.

Haim (Maccabi Tel Aviv), Khalilou Fadiga (Inter Milan), Les Ferdinand (Leicester City), Fernando Hierro (Real Madrid) and Radhi Jaidi (Esperance Tunis), went into the Charlton match with just two debutants. They were defender Julio Cesar, who had arrived from Real Madrid on loan, and veteran midfieldman Speed – the latter

Legend: former Real Madrid favourite Fernando Hierro brought a touch of class to the Bolton midfield.

boasted more experience in the League than any other player. Allardyce's own theory was that to compete in the top half of the table he needed a squad of 18 internationals and six highly-experienced players, rather than 18 experienced players and six up and coming players.

'Bringing Gary Speed in from Newcastle that summer was crucial, as was the loan signing of El-Hadji Diouf, because they both had vital Premier League experience, and we knew they would be able to cope with it physically and mentally,' says Allardyce.

The victory over Charlton set the tone for

Block: Jussi saves from Liverpool's Djibril Cisse.

an encouraging opening phase of the campaign. Defeat at Fulham was quickly made up for with wins at Southampton and at home to Liverpool. But the climb to the upper reaches of the League didn't go unnoticed. Newcastle United were suddenly looking for a new manager, and Allardyce was

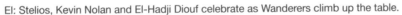

El: Stelios, Kevin Nolan and El-Hadji Diouf celebrate as Wanderers climb up the table.

a prominent name in the frame. As it turned out, Graeme Souness left Blackburn to take up the post when it was established that Sam was happy to continue his mission at the Reebok.

On the park, things were just as dramatic. In October, Manchester United snatched a point in a thrilling 2–2 draw at the Reebok. An injury-time goal by summer signing Les Ferdinand, aided and abetted by some comedy defending, appeared to have given Wanderers the home victory over the old enemy they so badly craved. But then David

Bellion went to the other end and bundled in an unwelcome equaliser. Allardyce still rates the spine-tingling reaction to Ferdinand's goal as one of the noisiest the stadium has witnessed in its entire 10 years.

'I think that was the peak of the crowd reactions here,' he says. 'When we went 2–1 in front, the celebrations made me tingle from top to bottom. It has happened on many occasions, but never quite as ferociously as that one. I couldn't hear something that was being said to me just three yards away. It was incredible. Unfortunately, we didn't hang on

Roof-raiser: Les Ferdinand scores to put Bolton ahead against United with just seconds remaining to send the Reebok crowd wild.

Gunning for you: Bolton defender Radhi Jaidi powers a header home at Arsenal to maintain Bolton's fine record against the Gunners.

to that famous victory and lost a goal in the dying seconds.'

Wanderers repeated the trick next time out at Arsenal, twice coming from behind to earn a point. Bolton's continued success was cherished at the Reebok but bitterly resented elsewhere. The major critics were losing rival managers who, one by one, complained about Bolton's approach to the game. The criticism tended to focus on an over-reliance on set pieces, a physical approach to the game and in some quarters the tactics were described in derogatory terms as simple long-ball.

Graeme Souness was typical. In October 2004, after Wanderers had beaten his Newcastle side 2–1 at the Reebok, he told the reporters in the post-match press conference 'You can complain about the fare that was on offer, in terms of passing and a good football match, but that is the way the games are here – you have to be up for the challenge. If you don't challenge, you are going to get bullied off the park.'

Allardyce, never one to back down from a fight, said Souness should concentrate on his own side. He believed the Bolton bashing was one part a diversionary tactic used by under-pressure managers to explain away poor results and one part media bias in favour of more fashionable clubs.

'Managers had to make excuses for the fact that Bolton Wanderers had beaten them,' he says. 'They had to do whatever they could to protect themselves and to protect their own jobs, simply because their fans and their board of directors didn't expect Bolton Wanderers to beat them. So, when we did beat them, they would say we did it a certain way, which either wasn't nice or good or correct or whatever.

'The thing is, people never expected us to sustain our success. For some, the very fact that Bolton Wanderers had become a successful team meant that the Premier League wasn't as good as it used to be, which was absolute nonsense. We were, and the club still is, relatively unfashionable, which doesn't help. Quite a lot of people who write in the media wanted to write about the fashionable sides. They didn't particularly want to write about the likes of Bolton.'

And, of course, Allardyce had science on his side. 'Our ProZone stats showed us the perception of how we play the game was not always matched by reality. Sides that were perceived to play in a better style than us – in terms of shorter passes – actually played more long balls than us. That was a fact. We were tagged 'a long-ball team', but we knew the true picture. Every time we play a game, ProZone highlights how many long passes we make. We do it, yes, but we do it to the teams we need to in order to beat them – we don't do it all the time or any more than other teams.'

Despite Allardyce's noisy protestations, the mud began to stick, but he didn't really lose too much sleep over it because after 12 games his side had collected an impressive 22 points. They were well placed in fourth behind Chelsea, Arsenal and that season's real surprise packet Everton.

But then the roof caved in. Without warning, Bolton went on a 10-game run when they couldn't buy a win.

Keeping it clean: Jussi Jaaskelainen, the clean-sheet master.

Recalls Forde, 'The first game in that cycle was against Aston Villa. I remember we had reserve goalkeeper Andy Oakes making his debut – it was highly unusual for Jussi to miss a game. El-Hadji had given us the lead, but Villa got one back before the break. Then the young German Thomas Hitzlsperger scored with a great strike in the 89th minute. But people forget that El-Hadji hit the post with a header with about five minutes to go. It could have been so different.

'I'll never forget collecting the newspapers the following day because I couldn't read the match reports, which is odd for me because I'm usually pretty objective. That defeat started the run. We drew at Chelsea, which was great, but then lost 3–2 at both Everton and Norwich. It was unusual for us to concede like that and even more unusual because we had been 2–1 up in both of those games. That was uncharacteristic for us as a club and uncharacteristic for Sam as a manager to have a run of results like that. The run just went on and on and we lost at home against Manchester City and Blackburn Rovers, and the mood in the stadium was deathly.'

By the time bottom-of-the-table West Brom arrived at the Reebok on New Year's Day 2005, the rot had well and truly set in. Bolton had lost six on the bounce in the Premier League – their worst run ever in the top flight – and in the process had slipped from fourth to 13th in the table, leaving the side closer to the relegation scrap than the European battle. The West Brom game was played in terrible weather conditions and the doom-laden skies seemed even more appropriate when the visitors took advantage of Wanderers' nervousness by scoring in the 13th minute.

'At times like these you look to your big players,' says Forde. 'If we'd have lost 1–0 that day, it would have made it seven straight defeats. But the mentality of the players in that last 15 minutes reached the point where, collectively and individually, they seemed to be sick of losing, sick of feeling a certain way, and they decided to change it.'

Ivan Campo took charge of the game, spraying passes around the park as Wanderers searched for an equaliser. Finally, with just five minutes remaining, the Spaniard's clever prompting paid off. He found Hunt with a defence-splitting ball down the right, and the Bolton-born full-back crossed into the Albion box. Diouf reacted the quickest to the ball and smashed it gleefully into the roof of the net.

It was a moment that turned a season. Suddenly, after staring into the abyss, Wanderers rediscovered the form that had seen them challenging for Europe early on. They reeled off five wins in the League and saw off Ipswich, Oldham and Fulham to reach the last eight of the FA Cup.

'I am not sure whether we would've taken a draw before the kick-off, but in the context of the game it was a brilliant result. We went

to Birmingham three days later and Kevin Nolan scored in the last minute in a 2–1 win,' says Forde.

'We have four phases in the season, that's what we work on. The first 10 games, the second 10, third 10 and last eight. It is amazing to reflect that the most successful season we had ever had in the Premier League in terms of points included our worst ever 10-game phase. In that run we collected just five points in 10 games. After the West Brom game we went on to get 23 points in 10 games, which was the backbone of the season.

Hero: Fernando Hierro's experience proved vital during the campaign.

I think coming back from that spell shows the resilience of the players and that resilience comes from the manager.'

At this stage Fernando Hierro – an undisputed legend of Spanish football and in many people's eyes the biggest name ever to pull on a Bolton shirt – started to show his class. As was club policy, Hierro hadn't been thrown into the action at the start of the season, despite his incredible CV. The Premier League is a different style of football than La Liga and even the greats need time to adjust to it. But when the push for Europe began in earnest that spring, Hierro showed why he had earned such exalted praise in his native land.

'All the players were magnificent,' says Forde. 'But Fernando was really incredible. It is interesting to note how the big personalities, the big star players, all seemed to roll their sleeves up and produce just when it was needed. It's not just fluke.'

By March, with 29 games gone, Wanderers had climbed back up to sixth spot, and the European dream, or rather plan, was back on track. But, despite the vastly improved fortunes, the memory of the winter of discontent was still fresh. What's more, that run had ensured that Bolton's margin for error in the remaining games was almost non-existent, particularly in games that, on paper at least, they were expected to win. Up next at the Reebok were relegation-threatened Norwich City.

'From our research we knew that the points you pick up against the teams that finish in the bottom eight are the cornerstones of a successful season. By that I mean qualifying for Europe,' says Forde. 'For example, if you look at the record books you'll find that in 2001 Ipswich Town got into the UEFA Cup with 66 points. What the books don't show you is that they won about 48 of those points in the 16 games against the bottom eight, which is an incredible tally. In 10 years no one has ever got anywhere close to that for a team that finished fifth. The best we've done is 31.

'But these are vital games. They are what we call the "mentality games". The matches when the stadium is perhaps only 80 or 85 percent full and the crowd are waiting for you to give them a lift. Prior to the visit of Norwich we had suffered a couple of indifferent games (an El-Hadji Diouf-inspired win at Manchester City was sandwiched between defeats at home to Arsenal in the FA Cup quarter-final and at Newcastle United in the League).

'Going into the game we knew what we had to do. We sat down with the appraisals of the players on the Monday and Tuesday beforehand, and we conducted them in the Chairman's Suite in the Reebok because we wanted to give the session a bit of an aura. The Chairman's Suite is a grand setting. One by one the players came in and sat down. Stelios first, then Fernando, Jay Jay and the others, and each of them talked about the significance of this particular game. They all knew that if we were going to be a true contender for Europe this was one of the games we had to win. It doesn't matter how you do it – nobody will be writing a book about games like these – you just have to do it and get the three points. Stelios knew that as much as anyone because of his Olympiakos background.

'Fernando always used to say when he was at Madrid that League games on the Saturday before big Champions League encounters were only about winning the game. You get 1–0 up, shut up shop, game over. For him, that was the ultimate in professionalism. Win the game at only 80 percent because the likes of Bayern Munich, Manchester United, Roma

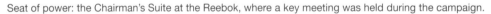

Seat of power: the Chairman's Suite at the Reebok, where a key meeting was held during the campaign.

or Inter Milan are turning up on Wednesday. Why bust a gut beating Real Mallorca or Getafe 5–0, when 1–0 will do?'

Against Norwich it wasn't a performance to remember, but it did include a goal to remember by the mercurial Greek international Stelios. Wanderers' attacks had been thwarted for much of the first half by emerging England international goalkeeper Robert Green, when in the 42nd minute they won a corner. Stelios picked up the ball on the edge of the box from a half-cleared corner. From the right-hand edge he curled a fabulous 25-yarder beyond the reach of Green into the top corner. With Bolton

failing to add to their lead, the nerves among supporters started to fray, but Hierro was majestic. He controlled the game, came close to scoring and ensured the points were safe. The 1–0 win took the side up to fifth in the table – within five points of fourth-placed Everton.

'The goal Stelios scored was special and so was the result because it was a huge game for us,' says Forde. 'The run of results started to energise and revive the squad. They grew and grew in confidence.'

Stelios was an important influence on the field and in the dressing room. If Wanderers needed a talisman, who represented what

Vital strike: Stelios (hidden) scores the winner against Norwich, a victory which was crucial to the team's confidence.

Saints alive: Stelios heads Bolton into the lead against Southampton to keep the European dream alive.

could be achieved with decent organisation and belief, he was the perfect role model. For in the summer of 2004 he had been part of the Greek national team that had stunned the football world by winning Euro 2004 in Portugal. Greece had started the tournament as rank outsiders and yet, thanks to a very carefully planned campaign, had triumphed. He was a man used to winning things. At Olympiakos he had collected seven successive League Championship-winning medals, as well as Greece's Player of the Year award. He too was a firm believer that Wanderers could learn from his national side's success story.

'Winning Euro 2004 was a dream, an impossible dream, but we did it and it became reality. It was a fantastic achievement,' he says. 'To be honest, we didn't go to Portugal to win the Cup, we went to try our best, play good football and enjoy ourselves. But we soon realised we could do something better. We believed in ourselves and showed that nothing is impossible in football. It's a philosophy, a mindset, and I think we have that at Bolton too. When people underestimate the team, it works in our favour. The thing is if you don't have dreams, if you don't have goals to fulfil, you are nothing.'

After the Stelios-inspired Norwich success, suddenly it wasn't just Europe that was on the agenda, there was now talk of a Champions League place. Back-to-back victories over Fulham then Charlton strengthened Wanderers' hopes. With fives games left to play, they found themselves just two points adrift of David Moyes's Everton and a point ahead of faltering Liverpool. With relegation-threatened Southampton set to visit the Reebok, Wanderers had a chance to go fourth. It was another of the mentality games.

'The game against Southampton was a massive one,' says Allardyce. 'We knew that if we could win it, we would go above Everton at least for a night because they were playing the following evening at Manchester United and that would have piled the pressure on them. The performance was right but not the result.'

Stelios gave Wanderers the lead midway through the first half as Wanderers put on one of their best performances of the season. They created several more good chances, but a combination of Antii Niemi in the Southampton goal and bad luck prevented Bolton from making the points safe. In the second half, Kevin Phillips grabbed an equaliser.

The Champions League hopes were all but dashed by that result, but Wanderers' European dream remained within touching distance. Gary Speed scored his first goal for the club in the next match, a battling 1–1 draw at Aston Villa. Bolton had three games to play, but Spurs and Middlesbrough, their closest rivals for Europe, were threatening to close in on them. Even so, Bolton knew that victory in their next game would be enough to secure sixth spot and with it a UEFA Cup place for the first time in the club's history. The only fly in the ointment was that the match was against Jose Mourihno's Chelsea, who wanted the three points to secure the Premier League title.

Wanderers' modest resources were in sharp relief to the mountain of wealth that had helped Chelsea to the brink of their first title in 50 years. Russian billionaire owner

It's your party: Chelsea players mob Frank Lampard as they close in on the title at the Reebok.

Roman Abramovich had spent well over £300 million to reach this stage, not only in buying the club but also wiping out the debts and rebuilding the entire squad.

What took place at the Reebok was a gripping but ultimately frustrating contest. Bolton lost 2–0 to two Frank Lampard goals. Drowned out amid the hoopla that surrounded Chelsea's title triumph at the final whistle were Allardyce's bitter complaints over the Londoner's opening goal. Referee Steve Dunn missed a blatant foul on Hierro in the build-up, yet the controversy was lost amid the sound of popping champagne corks.

Even now, Allardyce remains bitter about how Wanderers were treated that day. 'I was extremely unhappy at the way the game went. All week beforehand it was being billed as Chelsea's big match, but for us it was a far more important game because they were already so far in front they would have gone on to win the League anyway. That was never in doubt.

Passport control: El-Hadji Diouf puts Bolton in front at Portsmouth on the day the club qualified for the UEFA Cup.

'We were a small-town club, playing in the most elite League in the world against some of the most talented players. I believe that for a club of our size to win a place in the UEFA Cup was a bigger achievement than Chelsea winning the League, because Chelsea had done that before. But at that point in the entire 128-year history Bolton Wanderers had never been in Europe.'

Despite the Chelsea set-back, Wanderers remained in sixth place and with two games to go were three points ahead of Steve McClaren's Middlesbrough, who were playing Spurs. A point at Portsmouth would be enough to ensure a minimum of a

Finish line: Stelios scores a last-day winner over Everton to get Bolton's Euro party started.

seventh-place finish and with it European qualification.

Diouf, who had been in great form, gave Bolton an early lead at Fratton Park and, despite a late Yakubu equaliser, Wanderers did enough to create history. The final game of the season saw Everton visit the Reebok. It

Cheer we go: Big Sam leads the Reebok celebrations as Bolton look forward to their first European campaign.

was a thrilling finale to a marvellous campaign. One–nil down and reduced to 10 men at the break following the dismissal of Bruno N'Gotty, Wanderers produced a stirring fightback to win 3–2.

Bolton could reflect on a sixth-place finish in one of the toughest Leagues in the world. Their haul of 58 points matched Liverpool's, who only finished higher in the final standings on goal difference.

After the final whistle Allardyce summed it up: 'What we have achieved is sometimes overlooked, but when you step back and consider where we had come from it is absolutely incredible. Unfortunately, I think it will only be in the future that this period will be recognised for what it is worth. Only then will we truly be given the credit we deserve.'

So, what did Big Sam put Wanderers' rise down to?

'One of the keys to our success was the structure we were able to put in place. The research, the knowledge of the staff, that is the biggest factor.'

And, of course, there's the man with the plan.

Best 10 Signings Since The Reebok Stadium Opened

Claus Jensen
Mark Fish
Jussi Jaaskelainen
Ricardo Gardner
Jay Jay Okocha
Youri Djorkaeff
Fernando Hierro
Tal Ben Haim
Kevin Davies
Bruno N'Gotty

2004–05

Ins

Tal Ben Haim (Maccabi Tel Aviv), Vincent Candela (loan, Roma), El-Hadji Diouf (Liverpool), Khalilou Fadiga (Inter Milan), Les Ferdinand (Leicester City), Fernando Hierro (Real Madrid), Radhi Jaidi (Esperance Tunis), Julio Cesar (loan, Real Madrid), Blessing Kaku (FC Ashdod), Joey O'Brien (trainee), Andy Oakes (loan, Derby County), Gary Speed (Newcastle United), Ricky Shakes (trainee), Robert Sissons (trainee), Michael Bridges (Leeds United).

Outs

Anthony Barness (Plymouth Argyle), Ibrahim Ba (Çaykur Rizespor), Simon Charlton (Norwich City), Charlie Comyn-Platt (Swindon Town), Les Ferdinand (Reading), Youri Djorkaeff (Blackburn Rovers), Fernando Hierro (retired), Blessing Kaku (Maccabi Tel Aviv), Andy Oakes (loan, Derby County), Emerson Thome (Wigan Athletic), Per Frandsen (Wigan Athletic), Vincent Candela (loan, Roma), Julio Cesar (loan, Real Madrid), Michael Bridges (Sunderland).

Chapter Nine

We Have Lift Off

Scarborough. Famed for fish and McCain oven chips, it's the quintessential English seaside resort. A football super power, however, it most definitely ain't. Prior to the 1987–88 season Scarborough FC had spent its entire history as a non-League club but, having clinched the Conference title in '87, they were starting out on an exciting new journey. In stark contrast, Bolton Wanderers, proud founder members of the Football League, with history and tradition dating back more than 100 years, had sunk to a new low, relegated to the old Division Four, the bottom rung of the Football League's ladder, for the very first time in their history.

On 29 August 1987 the two clubs were due to meet at the McCain Stadium. For a club of Bolton's stature, things couldn't get much worse. Then Wanderers lost 4–0. Ouch.

Bolton fan Martin Dean was there that day. A grand day out, spoiled only by the football. Fast forward 18 years to the summer of 2005, and Martin found himself in another seaside resort, preparing for another Wanderers match.

This time, however, it was a little different, for Wanderers were in the Black Sea city of Burgas in Bulgaria. Allardyce and his side were there to take on Lokomotiv Plovdiv in the club's first ever UEFA Cup clash on foreign soil, and Dean, along with hundreds of other Wanderers diehards, was there for a match he just couldn't miss.

As the bright summer sun glistened on the waves outside the Marina bar, Martin found himself reminiscing about the dark days of Scarborough with faces from the past.

'People I hadn't seen for the best part of 20 years were there on the streets of that Bulgarian town. It was amazing. Everywhere you looked lads were there just grinning from ear to ear. It was incredible to think that we had made it!'

A month earlier Wanderers chairman Phil

Gartside had taken a European trip of his own. He had travelled to Monaco in order to represent the club when the draw for the first round of the UEFA Cup was made. It was an historic moment for Bolton Wanderers Football Club, and Gartside wanted to savour every single second.

'I wasn't going to miss that one for the world,' he says. 'It was a fantastic honour for me. I had been a supporter long enough to understand what it meant. It was the first time Bolton Wanderers had been involved, and I wanted to be there. I didn't really care who we were drawn against, it was just wonderful to be part of it. All the big guns of Europe were represented, and being there confirmed that we had arrived.'

The formalities, televised live and supervised by UEFA chief executive Lars-Christer Olsson, paired Wanderers with Lokomitv Plovdiv, the first leg to be played at the Reebok on 15 September – the return two weeks later.

Dean had been at home in London watching events unfold on TV. He summed up the feelings of most long-term supporters: 'When the draw was made, everyone was saying the same thing, "Where's Plovdiv? Who are they?" To be honest, the only Bulgarian club side I'd heard of were Sofia. But I think the mystery of the whole thing was all part of the excitement. Going into Europe was all new to us. And going to somewhere like Plovdiv was special, because we really were going into the unknown.'

Just as it was a new experience for the supporters, it was a journey into uncharted territory for Allardyce and his backroom team too. That said, the manager had set about preparing for the European challenge with all his customary thoroughness, nothing was left to chance. In pre-season, Wanderers had accepted an invitation, along with Everton and Manchester City, to take part in the Premier League Asia Trophy in Thailand. Unusually for Bolton, they actually enjoyed some pre-season success and won the tournament, but the trip was important too because it allowed the backroom staff to plan for the European trips that would follow that season.

Allardyce tasked the backroom boys with drawing up a plan that would allow them to get the most out of the playing staff who would have to face a tough campaign because of the extra games and the travelling that European football brings. The priority remained the Premier League and the staff had noted how teams – even those with much larger playing resources than Wanderers – had often struggled to cope with the demands of domestic football following a midweek European trip. Having enjoyed two relatively successful campaigns, Bolton were keen not to let their standards slip. Euro hangovers were something they were desperately keen to avoid. A measure of success of the club's European campaign would not just be the results in the UEFA Cup matches themselves, but also in how many points they managed to pick up in matches immediately after.

The solution the club hit on was to rest the players as much as possible and to look at ways of minimising the effects of all the travel. Various members of staff were sent to check out the hotels ahead of the games to ensure the accommodation suited their requirements. The club even sent a chef out to check that the food preparation was right. Unusually, Wanderers even elected to stay abroad the night of games – whereas traditionally clubs travelled back straight after. They also kept to English time throughout trips, so that the body clocks of the players didn't have to adjust.

Glove story: Japan star Hidetoshi Nakata joined Bolton to bolster the squad for the European games.

Allardyce retained the bulk of the squad that had qualified for Europe, but the playing ranks were beefed up by the additions of Mexican striker Jared Borgetti, who arrived from Pachuca for £1 million, and Hidetoshi Nakata, Japan's answer to David Beckham, who joined on a season-long loan from Fiorentina. Closer to home, Ian Walker arrived from Leicester City to bolster the goalkeeping department. As usual, the manager unearthed another bargain in the giant shape of Abdoulaye Faye, who was signed from Lens, initially on loan, though the deal was made permanent in January 2006. In contrast to the media scrum that surrounded Nakata's capture, Faye's was one of those typically unheralded signings. He came in under the radar and yet went on to make a huge impact almost as soon as he arrived.

Meanwhile, El-Hadji Diouf was signed on a permanent deal (reported to be around the £3 million mark) after his successful season-long loan from Liverpool. Though considerably less than the £10 million Liverpool had paid for him, it was still Wanderers' biggest fee since Dean Holdsworth had arrived from Wimbledon in 1997. As such, it also represented a loosening of the purse strings – a reward for Allardyce, who had dramatically transformed the club's fortunes.

These big-name players may not have arrived on huge transfer fees, but Wanderers were paying Premier League wages.

Says Chief Executive Allan Duckworth, 'You've got to treat it very much like any other entertainment business. Everyone knows that television and film stars are paid far more than anybody else who works in the studio. They are the stars of the show and you have to accept that. Before joining the club I'd never worked in a business like this before, but I rationalised the huge amounts the players get paid by seeing them as the product. Like any business, you invest money in your product, you improve your product and continually repackage your product. All your money goes into your product because that's what's going to bring your income in. The other way you spend money is on developing new products, hence the investment in the academy.'

While Wanderers had invested in the playing side, there had been the odd departure too, though probably the most significant was from the coaching ranks. Allardyce's trusted right-hand man Phil Brown had decided to leave the Reebok to take up the challenge of managing Derby County in June 2005.

To replace him, the manager turned to one of the most respected coaches in the business, Sammy Lee. As a player, Lee had made his name with the legendary Liverpool sides of the early 80s, collecting three League titles and two European Cups. He had actually turned out for Bolton too at the tail-end of his playing career, linking up with former Anfield teammate Phil Neal, who was the manager at the time. But injuries had restricted Lee to a handful of appearances.

In the interim, Lee had established a reputation as one of the most progressive coaches in the land. Prior to his arrival at the Reebok, he had been working with the England set-up and would continue to do so up until the end of the 2006 World Cup in Germany.

Wanderers' squad may have been small, but there was little doubt among the players that it was well formed. They firmly believed that the club deserved their new-found status as one of the nation's European standard

New face: Sammy Lee joined as assistant to manager Sam Allardyce.

bearers. Goalkeeper Jussi Jaaskelainen, who had been through all the highs and lows of the Reebok years, says, 'The first two years in the Premier League were all about survival, but during that time we also built up the backroom staff and made improvements to the training ground. Then we started to bring in better and more experienced players.

'I wasn't surprised when we eventually qualified for Europe. We managed it because, over time, the squad got better and better. There was a lot of pressure on the side when we were playing in the bottom three, much more than when we were trying to qualify for Europe. The one thing that also changed was the expectation levels – of the fans and the players. They went up too.

'But I certainly wasn't surprised by the success we had. We had finished eighth, then sixth and when you looked at the squad of

Do the Lokomotiv: Mexican striker Jared Borgetti ensures Bolton's first game in Europe ends in victory.

players, it was clear how we had managed it.'

What Jussi and his teammates needed was a half decent start to the League campaign and eight points from the first five games was just that. It meant that the historic first European game against Lokomotiv Plovdiv could be savoured rather than looked at as an unhelpful distraction.

As the Bulgarian side were an unknown quantity, chief scout Jack Chapman had been dispatched to check them out ahead of the tie. It may have been a bit of history, but Allardyce wasn't going to let that small detail cloud his judgement. His priority remained the Premier

League and Europe was a nice bonus. So, in line with that thinking and his plan to conserve the energies of players, he made four changes to the side that had been held by Blackburn Rovers in their previous outing. Nakata was given his first start, much to the delight of the Japanese media who were assigned *en masse* to cover the player's every move.

The historic encounter attracted a crowd of almost 20,000 and the received wisdom beforehand was that Wanderers' Premier League class would be far too much for the Bulgarians. But football rarely works like that. Despite an early onslaught, Wanderers failed to make the breakthrough and looked increasingly susceptible to Plovdiv's counter-attacks. It was no shock when Boban Janchevski grabbed a goal in the 28th minute for the visitors.

Just when it seemed as though Wanderers' first taste of European football would be a bitter one, Bolton scored a stunning equaliser. Nicky Hunt's cross from just inside the Plovdiv half was met by a diving header from Diouf. In the second minute of injury time the fightback was complete when Nakata teed up Borgetti and the Mexican drove the ball in from 12 yards.

Two weeks later, with Wanderers now up to third in the League, they headed off to Bulgaria to complete the job.

Martin Dean was part of a group of supporters who were making a flying visit for the match. In all, three plane loads of fans took off for Bulgaria on Thursday 29 September 2005.

'On the day of the game we were up at something like 4am to get to Manchester airport,' he says. 'Right from the start this wasn't like going to a normal game. Everyone was excited. We knew we were part of something special. It was an adventure. You

White army: Wanderers fans savouring the atmosphere ahead of the club's first ever European away game.

could see it in everyone's face on the plane as we took off. It was an event that we simply didn't want to miss. Everyone knew it was the first [Bolton game away in Europe] and it could have been the last. Nobody could say at that point. If we had lost that night, we would have gone out. It had taken us 128 years to qualify for Europe in the first place, so who knows how long it would take for it to come round again.

'When we touched down in Bulgaria, there were coaches waiting to transfer us to Burgas, where we had something to eat and a couple of drinks. As we walked around we kept bumping into Bolton people, some I hadn't seen for years, men who had been young lads on the terraces with me at places like Burnden and at Darlington and Scarborough. That match at Scarborough was the worst result ever for me. They had just come into the Football League and we…well we were just poor. And now we were in Europe. It was incredible really.'

The supporters deserved their place in the sun, for without their loyalty and generosity to the club over the years the Allardyce revolution might never have happened. Money raised by fans through the Bolton

Wanderers Development Association's combined lotteries – Lifeline, Goldline, scratch tickets, Golden Gamble and the e-lottery – had enabled the Bolton boss to finance his dream of turning the club into a leading Premier League side.

There are specific rules regarding the association's fundraising pot. It pays for projects which are designed to enhance the club for fans and players alike. From new training areas at Euxton to the concourse bins at the Reebok, the association has been there. Between 2000 and 2007 it provided more than £3.6 million for a huge variety of club projects.

Martin Dean's father, Andrew Dean, is the promotions manager in charge of all the associated draws as well as a small army of agents. He says 'Not only do members have the chance to win a big cash prize, but their money is put to use for their benefit in other ways. There are a number of projects that the Lifeline lottery has helped pay for, like improving disabled facilities or upgrading the big screen. We look at the things fans want to see to improve the stadium and try to deliver.'

Allardyce has been a long-term supporter

of the lotteries – remember this was the guy who used to go round collecting club funds with the priest when he was a manger in Ireland – in fact, since his playing days he had been a member. But, more importantly, he knew how the system worked and how to appeal for the funds that would help him do his job, particularly at a time when finances were tight. For example, in February 2001 it helped pay for ProZone, one of the key technological systems which helped the team stay one step ahead of the opposition.

'The development at the training ground was made possible by the lotteries,' says Allardyce. 'The funds enabled us to bring the junior and senior sections under one roof; develop a high-spec, fully-integrated training complex; incorporate a sports science centre, video analysis and ProZone statistics, which together help the players perform better. These facilities helped the team compete at the highest level.'

Back in Burgas, Martin Dean was happy to savour the moment. As Wanderers supporters go, the 37-year-old is Premier League class. A lifelong fan, he is a dealer in football memorabilia and has almost every single Wanderers programme going back to

the mid 1950s. He's an engaging, intelligent man with a passion for the football club that is in his genes.

'Watching Bolton is just part of my life, always has been. It's in the blood. I can remember being at my first game with my dad and grandad.' Dean can instantly recall the date, opponents and score. 'League Cup, September 1975, Coventry City, lost 3–1. Byrom scored for us.'

For him the journey to Bulgaria had taken 30 years.

'When we were struggling in Divisions Three and Four, if anyone had told me that less than 20 years later we would be in Europe, I would have laughed at them. It was unthinkable. Burnden Park had become a mess. It had a supermarket in one corner which had ruined the character of the place. It was sad to see it like that. I was delighted about us going to a new stadium. I have some great memories from Burnden Park, but it was time to move on.'

Dean's Burgas nostalgia trip was brought to an end when the coaches arrived to take supporters to the game.

'The Bulgarians were wonderfully friendly. The coach driver had even brought along some beers which he had put in the luggage hold. He sold them to supporters as they got on his coach, which helped international relations no end!'

The second-leg venue was the Naftex Stadium, more than 200 miles from Plovdiv, as Lokomotiv's ground had failed to meet UEFA standards.

Around 1,500 Wanderers fans had made the trip and, with Wanderers 2–1 up from the first leg, there were few grumbles when Wanderers took to the field, despite seven changes to the side that had played in the previous League game. Borgetti, Fabrice Fernandes, Ian Walker and Joey O'Brien, who was fresh out of the club's academy, were each handed first starts.

Viewed by some as a selection gamble, it was part of the manager's ploy to get the most out of his squad on all fronts. However, when Georgi Iliev smashed the ball home from long range on 51 minutes, the tie was level on aggregate and Plovdiv had the advantage on an away goal. The tinkering looked as though it may prove costly. Wanderers needed to score. Time was running out and, until going behind, Bolton had rarely threatened a shot, let alone a goal. As the clock ticked down,

Lady Luck, or rather hapless Plovdiv defender Aleksandar Tunchev, intervened. Tunchev turned a cross into his own goal when there were no Wanderers players around. Kevin Nolan then put the icing on the cake with a winner five minutes from time.

From the terraces, the match itself was a sideshow to the main event – atmosphere sampling. 'It was totally different to anything we were used to,' says Dean. 'There were firecrackers and fireworks going off and the Plovdiv supporters were fascinating to listen to. The whole day had been fantastic. We really had got a taste for the European adventure. So when we went behind, we desperately wanted Bolton to score – not simply for pride or whatever – but so that we could qualify for the group games and the adventure would continue. Kevin Nolan came on and made a big difference on the night.'

Safely through, the draw for the group paired Wanderers with Besiktas from Turkey, Russian outfit Zenit St Petersburg, Portuguese side Guimaraes and emerging Spanish force Sevilla. The latter and Zenit would visit the Reebok, while Wanderers would have to travel to Besiktas and

Going Loko: supporters and players go wild as Bolton level the scores in Bulgaria.

Flying high: Bolton players mob scorer Kevin Nolan as they come from behind to complete the victory.

Young hopeful: academy graduate Joey O'Brien, pictured in action in Besiktas, was to have an impressive first season for the club.

Guimaraes. Three out of the five sides would qualify for the last 32 stage. The first test was to be a trip to Istanbul to take on Besiktas.

'Again, the draw for the group stages didn't really matter to me, I would have happily gone anywhere. But the first trip was to Besiktas and quite a few people were a little bit wary of going there because of reports of other British clubs having trouble in Turkey in the past. But I never gave it a moment's thought.

'Everyone was buzzing again as we went for the early morning flight. I was sat next to

a middle-aged guy and his son and this was a special trip for them – they'd saved up for it. When we landed, we went into the city. It was bitterly cold so we made a beeline for a bar that had welcomed Wanderers fans. They'd let us hang Bolton flags up without a problem and there wasn't a hint of trouble. When we came across any Turkish football fans all they wanted to talk about was Jay Jay Okocha, because he had played for Fenerbahce, another Istanbul club.

'My dad and I went off for a shave in a Turkish barber's shop and later we had a drink with the chairman Phil Gartside, who had found the fans' bar.'

'All the usual stuff you talk about on away trips like who would play or who wouldn't never occurred to me. Watching the Besiktas fans was amazing. They had a guy who was acting as a conductor. When he raised his right arm the fans on the right-hand side of the ground would all sing and then when he raised his left, the left-hand side would join in. It was pure theatre.'

On the park a much changed Wanderers side maintained their European record of falling behind in games. But Borgetti, who had rarely figured in Premier League matches, showed his class with a clinical piece of finishing to earn Wanderers a point.

'It was a group match, so to be honest I hadn't been too worried about the result. Getting a draw just made the day even better. Of course, we felt it was a good result, because we knew that traditionally most teams struggled playing in Turkey because their supporters are so passionate there.'

Wanderers gave themselves an excellent chance of qualifying for the knockout stages when they beat Russian side Zenit St Petersburg 1–0 at the Reebok in November

Pen pal: Gary Speed takes time out from a training session to sign a shirt.

thanks to a goal from Kevin Nolan, who had assumed the captaincy in the absence of Gary Speed. It was a foul night, with driving, heavy rain forming pools of water on the field, making the closing action almost farcical. If it had been a regular League game there's every chance that it would have been abandoned, but asking Zenit to make the round trip to Bolton twice clearly weighed on the officials' minds.

The trip to Portugal was the one many Bolton fans had earmarked as 'the' trip to make. It wasn't a trip, more a mass invasion. In addition to the official travellers, hundreds more made their own way independently and all told some 3,000 Wanderers fans went to Guimaraes. Among them, of course, was Martin Dean. Though his early scouting missions in Bulgaria and Turkey hadn't prepared him for what he found in the north west of Portugal.

Making a splash: Bolton star Jay Jay Okocha struggles to keep his feet during the rain-soaked game against Zenit.

Vaz Lane: Ricardo Vaz Te takes the plaudits after scoring a stunner in his native Portugal.

'The scene when we got into the main square in Guimaraes (a UNESCO World Heritage site) was incredible. It was like a Wembley Cup Final. There were old cobbled squares just teaming with Bolton supporters. As the day progressed, fans were knocking on doors and asking the locals if they would hang flags out of their windows and off their balconies. They did, and the whole place looked fantastic. The atmosphere was great. Supporters were singing all the old songs.

'Once again, I was bumping into people who I hadn't seen for years, from Great Lever, Farnworth, Horwich – all there in this tiny square, names forgotten but not faces. There was even a bond between complete strangers. Everyone you looked at had a smile on their face. It was like being at one huge party. It is a feeling I will never forget.

'The locals just looked at us as though we had come from another planet! There was a real holiday atmosphere. I felt really proud to be there and be part of it.'

At the ground, the party continued, fuelled by non-alcoholic beer. Many Bolton fans were so well partied by that point they had little idea what they were drinking. As for the football, it followed a now familiar pattern.

Wanderers fell behind, though this time with only five minutes left. Thankfully, they came storming back. Youth star Ricardo Vaz Te, on an emotional return to his native Portugal, fired home a Goal of the Season contender to level things three minutes from time. The terrace party continued well into the night – though some of the hangovers will have been a little less fierce than usual.

The result left Wanderers needing a point in their final group game at home to Sevilla to ensure qualification for the last 32 of the competition. They warmed up for it by beating Arsenal 2–0 at the Reebok. Sevilla, however, proved to be a tougher nut to crack. Bolton had to settle for a 1–1 draw. They had gone in front through veteran defender Bruno N'Gotty, only for Sevilla to level in the second half. The knockout draw paired

Faye day: Abdoulaye Faye scores against Arsenal.

Wanderers with N'Gotty's old club, French giants Marseille.

'When Marseille came out of the hat, it felt like we had arrived,' says Dean. 'They were a big-name club with a real European pedigree. Unlike some of the other sides we had played up until then, people knew a little bit about Marseille. We had heard of the ground, the Stade Vélodrome, and they had won the Champions League in the 1990s before the financial scandals. They also had players, like the former Manchester United 'keeper Fabian Barthez, who we were familiar with.'

The Marseille match was scheduled for February, allowing Allardyce to concentrate on the League. At home the campaign was once again shaping up well, and Wanderers had coped impressively with the twin demands. They had even reached the quarter-finals of the Carling Cup, only to crash out after a disappointing display at Wigan.

On New Year's Day 2006 a packed Reebok saw Wanderers twice take the lead against Liverpool, only to be pegged back for a 2–2 draw. It kept the side in seventh place, and European qualification for a second successive season was a distinct possibility.

But Wanderers resources were being put under severe strain. The African Nations Cup in Egypt between 20 January and 10 February meant that the club would have to cope without El-Hadji Diouf, Abdoulaye Faye, Jay Jay Okocha and Radhi Jaidi. When Ivan Campo suffered a broken foot as Wanderers knocked Arsenal out of the FA Cup in January, the squad was weakened even further. Short-term deals that brought Matt Jansen from Blackburn Rovers and Oscar Perez from Cordoba during the January transfer window barely papered over the cracks.

If Wanderers' immediate playing resources were a headache for Allardyce, there was soon to be an added distraction for the Bolton boss. For the back pages of the national press were dominated in January by reports of what England manager Sven-Göran Eriksson had said to an undercover reporter disguised as a wealthy Arab. In the immediate aftermath, the FA said that Eriksson's tenure as England boss would end after that summer's World Cup, a move that appeased those calling for the Swede's head, and one that signalled the start of the search for his successor.

Allardyce, who had won an army of

admirers for his work with Bolton, was immediately in the frame. He was mentioned whenever the vacancy was discussed. There were some who didn't like Wanderers' playing style, but his track record in man management, his astute signings, his reputation as being one of the game's most progressive thinkers and the stress he placed on preparation all counted in his favour. So too did his birth certificate. For, as the Eriksson era ended, there was a popular clamour to appoint an Englishman to manage England.

Reebok chairman Gartside made it clear he would be happy to see Allardyce take charge of the national side. He was far less happy when in February Newcastle parted company with Graeme Souness and his manager was, once again, linked with the Tyneside giants.

Amid all the potential distractions, the team managed to continue to churn out decent results as the Marseille game loomed large.

Wanderers had the better of a tight first leg, only to be denied a clear penalty when Marseille defender Frederic Dehu pushed away a Jay Jay Okocha cross which looked destined for Jared Borgetti. Still they hadn't conceded an away goal and travelled to France a week later on course for the last 16. Unfortunately, it wasn't a trip to remember for all sorts of reasons.

'After the party in Portugal the game in Marseille was completely different,' says Martin Dean. 'It was the worst European trip of the lot. Everything about the organisation over there seemed to be done to aggravate us. We never struck up any rapport with the French, and their police were quite frustrating. Before the game our coaches were taken to a warehouse in the middle of nowhere and we had to wait for an hour or so. They wouldn't even let us off for a comfort stop. That kind of thing dampened the atmosphere and things didn't improve when we got to the ground. We had heard a lot about the Stade Vélodrome and seen it on TV for big European games. But when we got there, we discovered we had one of the worst views I have ever known in all my years watching football.

'We were stuck high up in a corner behind fences, with concrete slabs to sit on, the only ground worse than that was Derby County's in the early 1990s.

'The Marseille crowd was very passionate.

They made plenty of noise and had lots of flags on display which helped pick the night up. We scored in the first half [through Stelios] but then they got level just before half-time and the place went berserk. It really lifted their crowd. I think if we could have held out and gone in at half-time leading, we could have maybe gone through.'

Wanderers fans were probably grateful of their poor view when, midway through the second period, a Ben Haim own-goal tipped the balance in favour of Marseille. And although Wanderers battled for an equaliser, it wasn't to be their night.

Heading to France, both supporters and players had harboured vague hopes of silverware and European glory. Now the adventure had come to an abrupt end. The disappointment for the players was clear from their body language as they trooped off the field. It was palpable too among the travelling supporters as the realisation hit home that Marseille was the end of the road.

'After the experiences we had enjoyed along the way, we just wanted it to go on and on. We were all absolutely gutted when we went out that night. But at the same time, I felt proud that we had made it through to

the last 32 and we had enjoyed four good trips.

'You never know when or even whether it will ever happen again.'

Despite the draining effects of the defeat and the journey, Wanderers lifted themselves for the visit of Fulham on the Sunday to win 2–1 and go sixth in the table. The careful planning and preparation had paid off to some degree. At that stage, with games in hand on their nearest rivals, the side remained well placed to secure European football once again. For players like Nicky Hunt and Kevin Nolan, who had come through the ranks, it was something they were keen to taste again. In mid March, after West Ham knocked the side out of the FA Cup, European qualification became the entire focus of the campaign.

At that point, with three quarters of the season gone, it seemed a good bet that Wanderers could do it.

However, throughout this time the speculation over the England manager's position refused to go away. As the weeks had passed, Allardyce had been installed as one of the bookies' favourites to land the job, along with Martin O'Neil, Phil Scholari and Steve

End of the road: Kevin Nolan troops off dejected following Bolton's European exit in Marseille.

McClaren. While the nation's phone-in fans debated the emerging candidates credentials, Wanderers were left to ponder the serious possibility of life after Big Sam.

Allardyce made no secret of the fact that he desperately wanted the job. At last his achievements at the Reebok came under serious scrutiny and, while he didn't win over every single critic, he started to receive some long overdue respect.

Presiding over Bolton's most successful era for almost 50 years may not have meant too much outside of the town, but the manner of that success – on a relative shoestring, with innovative thinking and strong man-management skills – was hitting home.

He was interviewed for the job and by all accounts put on an impressive presentation to the FA's panel. In April news broke that the FA were going to go for the big man. Allardyce, however, wasn't it. They wanted Brazilian 'Big' Phil Scolari. Almost as soon as the news broke, the FA was left to look red-faced as Scolari turned them down.

It came down to McClaren against Allardyce for the England job. But for the latter the timing was appalling. Wanderers hit the crest of a slump. Five successive defeats saw them sink to eighth. They were in danger of going out of contention for a European place altogether – despite having been in the hunt all season. By contrast, McClaren, who at Christmas was having season tickets thrown at him by disgruntled Middlesbrough fans, had engineered a Riverside revival and steered his side to the Final of the UEFA Cup and semi-final of the FA Cup.

In May 2006 the two men came head to head at the Reebok. By now, McClaren's forthcoming appointment was the FA's worst-kept secret. To add insult to injury, Wanderers were held to a 1–1 draw. The two points dropped meant Bolton went into the final game of the season knowing that they needed a win and a Newcastle slip-up in order to grab seventh spot and, with it, the final European place.

End game: Steve McClaren winks at the cameras after beating Big Sam to the England manager's job.

Allardyce was informed by FA chief executive Brian Barwick, before the final game of the season, that he hadn't got his dream job. 'He did not tell me why,' he said.

Four days later, Newcastle beat champions Chelsea so that Bolton's final day victory over Birmingham turned out to be a futile one. Wanderers finished eighth, missing out on Europe by one place.

And so, a season that had promised so much – history, adventure and more glory – had ended in falling flat. For supporters it meant there wouldn't be an immediate return trip to Europe, but there was the consolation, at least, that Big Sam, who had masterminded the first, would still be around. They could also take comfort from the fact that Bolton had finished in the top 10 of English football for a third successive season – a feat only achieved by four other clubs, namely Chelsea, Manchester United, Arsenal and Liverpool.

Wanderers were keeping exalted company. But for Allardyce this latest defeat against McClaren was one he would find difficult to shake off.

Talking points

1. Gerry Taggart's goal
2. Youri signs
3. The Arsenal comeback
4. Final whistle v Middlesbrough
5. Big Sam quits
6. Ivan's hair
7. The Zenit storm
8. Jay Jay's flicks
9. Diouf's antics
10. Mike Riley

2005–06

Ins

Ali Al Habsi (Lyn Oslo), Jared Borgetti (Pachuca), Martin Djetou (Fulham), Abdoulaye Faye (FC Lens), Fabrice Fernandes (Southampton), Hidetoshi Nakata (loan, Fiorentina), Matt Jansen (Blackburn Rovers), Ian Walker (Leicester City).

Outs

Fabrice Fernandes (Beitar Jerusalem), Martin Djetou (FC Istres), Florent Laville (FC Bastia), Jay Jay Okocha (Qatar Sports Club), Kevin Poole (Derby County), Ricky Shakes (Swindon Town).

Taking Charge

One evening, after a game, owner Eddie Davies, chairman Phil Gartside and a reporter were leaving the Reebok through the main entrance. Gartside, by now a familiar figure at the club, was approached by supporters and asked to sign a programme, while the silver-haired Davies and the reporter passed through the throng anonymously.

Davies laughs happily at the thought. 'It's the way I like it,' he says. 'I don't want to be recognised. I am not here for the kudos, I am here to enjoy myself. Anyway there's a downside to kudos that I don't want. I would rather concentrate on what I am really here for rather than positioning myself where I am not interested in being. I get my enjoyment from watching the football – full stop. That's what it is all about as far as I am concerned. You get the enjoyment of being successful both in technical terms on the pitch and financially.'

Since 1999 Davies has played an increasingly important role at Bolton Wanderers. According to Gartside and chief executive Allan Duckworth, the multi-millionaire businessman has been the saviour of Wanderers, but throughout that period he has never sought the limelight.

Unlike the Glaziers at Manchester United and Roman Abramovich at Chelsea, Davies assumed control of the club relatively quietly. Preferring to stay out of the limelight, Davies is a football club owner who shuns publicity.

Despite a glittering career in business that has taken him all over the world, Davies has never lost his Bolton accent, nor has he ever forgotten his roots. Born in Little Lever, his father was a packager, his mother a nurse. Like his classmates in the early 1950s, he was football mad and despite his lack of height he was a promising goalkeeper

'In those days when you were still at primary school you used to watch Bolton on one Saturday and Bury the following week, because we lived in Little Lever which was midway between the two towns. My dad was a Bolton Wanderers supporter so I was a Bolton Wanderers supporter. That's how life was,' says Davies, his eyes sparkling at the memory.

'I can't remember the first game I went to, but one of the first that sticks in my memory is the FA Cup Quarter Final match between Wolves and Bolton in 1958 at Burnden Park. Bolton won 2–1.'

As a youngster on matchdays Davies had his own ritual. 'I used to stand by the scoreboard on the railway embankment and

would take with me a block of wood, a sheet of wood, a screw and a screwdriver. When I got to my spot, I used to screw the block of wood onto the sheet of wood so I could stand on the block and look over everyone else's head.'

After primary school Davies progressed to Farnworth Grammar School and continued to play football alongside his studies.

'I played for Farnworth Boys' team and for the Bolton Boys' Federation. We trained with Bolton Wanderers on odd occasions at Bromwich Street [the old training ground] with the A team.'

From Farnworth Grammar, Eddie went on

In charge: Big Sam in discussion with Bolton Wanderers owner Eddie Davies.

to Durham University, where he earned a first-class degree in mathematics. A successful career in commerce then took him around the world, and at one point he headed a multi-national organisation's South American operation.

He continued to follow the fortunes of Wanderers from a distance via newspaper reports until he eventually settled on the Isle of Man; his wife Susan is a native of the island.

'I always used to try to watch Wanderers in the FA Cup because they were a good cup team. Sue had never been to a professional game in her life, so I took her to see Bolton play in the Cup away at Wolverhampton Wanderers one year. We won 2–0.'

In 1984 Davies linked up with an inventor to start Strix, a company whose controls and connectors in small domestic appliances are used by around 20 percent of the world's population. It was the first of a string of successful businesses he has been involved in. 'Strix has since been sold twice, and although I still retain a small shareholding I am not involved in it at all. But I have other businesses around the world that occupy me. Ten years ago I was flying 200,000 miles a

year, but you are electronically connected now so I might fly 50,000. I am now non-executive director in all of my businesses. As you go up the evolutionary curve, I am 60 years old now, you decide that's what you want to do.'

The seeds of Davies's arrival at the club were first sown at Old Trafford of all places.

'In one of the businesses that I had in the mid 1990s there was a chap called Professor Sir Roland Smith who used to work for me. He was chancellor at UMIST and, of course, he was also the chairman at Manchester United.'

This is how Davies came to be a guest of Sir Roland when Wanderers visited Old Trafford in September 1995 for a Premier League game. For the record, United won 3–0 but, as so often is the case in football, it was events in the boardroom that day which would have a major bearing on Wanderers in the years ahead.

'In the boardroom after the match I was talking to the Bolton Wanderers directors and I remember meeting Phil Gartside. They were talking about building the new stadium and they were making announcements about how they were going to build the stadium debt free. I said to Phil at that time "I think you are talking absolute rubbish. When you get in trouble give me a ring." A few years later, in 1999, I got a phone call in the office and my secretary said that Phil Gartside was on the line for me. I picked the phone up and said "Hi Phil. I know exactly what you're going to say." So we had a meeting and that's really how I got back involved in the club. It wasn't something I'd particularly been looking for. At the time the business [Wanderers] was technically bankrupt. We had to turn that position around. In 1999 the club was only surviving on the goodwill of the banks. Now we are solvent and the club has value.'

One of his first acts was to sign a cheque for £1 million, and he was rewarded with a seat on the Wanderers board.

'I viewed it as an investment like any other investment – it just happens that this is one of my hobbies too. I was given a position on the board because basically if you are going to invest so much money in a club, you want to know what they are going to do with it.'

Four years later Davies was given full control of the club's parent company, Burnden Leisure, having invested an estimated £14 million in the club (though he prefers not to discuss the figures in detail). At the meeting, a few shareholders expressed concern about the votes to transfer power to such a relatively low-key figure.

'Yes, there were a few objectors. But given that we had 94.5 percent voting in favour of it, you have to say only a few. I can understand their anxiety – ill-founded though it was – but they simply didn't understand the technicalities. The fact of the matter is their shareholdings were apparently diluted, but actually it meant nothing, because if I hadn't converted those loans in 2003 this club would have folded up. You can't dilute a nothing! What happened in 2003 was purely a technical exercise. By that stage I owned the club, *de facto* anyhow. I think we effectively owned the club from about 2000. The share exercise in 2003 was merely a technical one just to rationalise the position. It is as simple as that.'

Right from the start of his involvement in the club, Davies has insisted that Wanderers be run no differently to any of the other businesses he has been involved with. 'This is a hobby for me. But we run the club on business principles. Why not?

Light show: Wanderers versus Liverpool under the Reebok lights.

'What this club has been better at than other clubs in the League is resource management – using your resources to the best effect – which is what any business is all about anyway. The building of the stadium wrecked the club's finances. The stadium probably cost £10 million more than it should have done and was instrumental in causing the near bankruptcy of the club. But I also think from a resource management point of view – if you were to measure the financial management of the organisation – we were running at about two out of 10. It is now at about seven. You will never get 10 in any business, and in my experience I have never seen a nine. But there are eights available'

So, what does resource management actually mean? 'There are clubs in the League that have outstanding players available to them, but they cannot get a result out on the pitch, whereas we have got genuinely good players and we can get results on the pitch because of good management. That is not just good management in the sense of Sammy Lee or Sam Allardyce, it is good management of the whole of the club. There is an entire pyramid of people under Sammy

who get those players on the pitch each Saturday. Some are technical such as the coaches, physios, psychologists and so on. Then there are the admin people, the finance people, the hotel people and so on. They all help get that team out on the pitch.'

As non-executive director of the club, Davies leaves the day-to-day running to the chairman and chief executive. 'I have a management team headed by Phil [Gartside] and Allan [Duckworth], and they make all the tactical decisions. Anything strategic, we talk about. Generally their recommendations are sound.'

The strategy Davies has overseen has helped move Wanderers forward, and he is delighted with the progress.

'We have made a profit ever since we have been in the Premier League. In fact, we have rewritten the business model for football. At that time there was a big furore about how we were operating. But what we said was the business model everyone else in football was using was completely unsustainable from a financial point of view. So what we decided to do was look for Bosmans [players out of contract], loan players and only took players on short-term contracts, so that if we were to get relegated we wouldn't be carrying the cost burden down with us.

'I don't think it is a particularly enlightened way of behaving – it's what any good business would do. But let's face it this sport has to come out of the Dark Ages. In 1999 there were only three or four clubs making a profit. That sums up the lack of enlightenment that existed. Now, more than half the clubs make a profit so now that enlightenment is improving.'

The success of that strategy and the success on the field have meant that Davies has been able to deliver better quality players.

'In 1999 we were offloading people at a rate of knots. It is only recently that we have been able to loosen the financial reins – which has allowed us to buy players like Nicolas Anelka. That signing came about because the club could afford it.' It also came about because of Davies's expansive business network. 'I have contacts in Turkey – people who work for me there. We were able to do the deal over and above everyone else's heads because we could do it in Turkish and other people couldn't.'

The arrival of Anelka in August 2006 – at the start of the 2006–07 season – certainly was a watershed moment in the history of Bolton Wanderers. It wasn't so much a transfer as a statement of intent, a release from the financial shackles that, ironically, had helped the club to make its name.

The deal itself completely shattered the club transfer record as Wanderers paid £8m to Turkish side Fenerbahce for the striker. Anelka was still only 27 when he put pen to paper on a relatively long-term, four-year deal. Davies was effectively rewarding Allardyce for his efforts in establishing the club in the Premier League.

However, for the hard-headed businessman and expert mathematician, there is a practical limit to the largesse. He won't spend for the sake of it. He'll only do it if it adds up.

'Our long-term vision is: one, to keep the club in the Premier League; two, to make sure we are in the top half of the League; and three, to compete in Europe. As far as getting into the Champions League is concerned, well it would be nice, but the simple mathematics are that we would have to spend £100 million to move up from fifth position to fourth. This would mean investing in the team and carrying an enormous wage bill which this club simply cannot support.

New arrival: Nicolas Anelka presented to the press by Sam Allardyce.

'If we do get in because of our playing and managerial ability, great – but we cannot go out and spend the £100 million. It is purely a monetary situation, and unless you have got someone like Abramovich who is prepared to come in and spend £500 million (and still not win everything in sight) then you have to face facts. There are no other clubs around that I can see who are going to do it unless some investors come in who are prepared to spend that kind of money.'

That said, Anelka's arrival, and a significant bid prior to that for striker Andy Johnson, who eventually chose to go to Everton, underline the progress that has been made.

Allardyce was no longer 'gambling' on players. Anelka, who had left Arsenal almost 10 years earlier for £22 million on his way to Real Madrid, arrived at Bolton with a degree of baggage, part of which was a suitcase full of medals. Along with Premier League and FA Cup-winners' silverware from his Arsenal days, he won the European Championship with France, a Champions League title with Real Madrid, the Intertoto Cup with Paris Saint-Germain and the Turkish Premier Super League with Fenerbahce.

'It was an unprecedented amount of money for us, and it underscored the club's ambition,' says Allardyce. 'It was the biggest transfer I had done and the biggest transfer this club had ever done. It underlined the commitment of the directors and the owner. They had been 100 percent behind me since I joined the club. We'd always worked very well together and that's why there was a lot of success and a lot of good things happening at the club. I am not simply talking about what you see out on the pitch but behind the scenes too – in terms of reducing the massive debt that was here when I first took over. Of course, the success that we managed to bring to Bolton Wanderers meant that the investment got better and better, bigger and bigger – and the Anelka transfer was the biggest of the lot!'

Turning down overtures from both France and Germany, Anelka wanted to return to the English game, where he had first established his reputation. But from day one he made it clear he also wanted European football too. What was music to Bolton fans' ears was the fact that he believed he could satisfy that ambition at the Reebok.

'I like England because of the way the game is played – I like the style, the pace of the game and the fans,' Anelka told reporters. 'I like everything about England. So that's why, when I wanted to leave Fenerbahce, I wanted to come back to England. I saw Bolton last season, and they played great, finishing eighth, and I knew it was a good club. The club has a lot of very good players and they play good football. We have a big challenge together and everybody wants to be in Europe. I came here because I want to try to play in Europe next season.

'I could have gone to clubs in France or Germany, but I wanted to come back to England,' he adds. 'I decided to come to Bolton because they came to me first. I know Sam is a big manager here, and when he spoke to me it led to coming back to England.'

Anelka was joining a Bolton side that had got their Premier League campaign off to a decent start with a home win against Spurs, thanks to early goals from Kevin Davies and Ivan Campo, though he watched from the dugout at Charlton as Wanderers suffered their first defeat.

Anelka's debut came in the game against Watford at the Reebok – but it was the boot of Speed that earned the point, the veteran Welshman holding his nerve to score the only goal from the penalty spot deep into stoppage time. Anelka grabbed his first goal for the club in a League Cup win at Walsall on Tuesday 19 September.

That particular match was completely overshadowed by a BBC *Panorama* programme which was aired the same night.

In it, the undercover film showed two agents claiming they had made illegal payments to Allardyce. The manager's son Craig was caught up in the controversy too. He was filmed boasting about how he could get access to his father to do deals for Bolton, and was accused by the programme of receiving secret payments.

The following day Allardyce came out fighting, telling reporters camped outside his house 'I deny all allegations that have been alleged against me. The matter is in the lawyers' hands and will be resolved by due process. As a father, of course, it is painful to watch your son talk tall and exaggerate his influence for financial gain. If there is any real evidence – and there won't be, as I am utterly innocent of any wrongdoing – I would expect the BBC to give that evidence to both the FA

Perfect start: Kevin Davies heads Bolton into an early lead against Spurs on the opening day of the season.

Now we're flying: Ivan Campo is mobbed after scoring a goal against Liverpool.

and the [Premier League's] Quest inquiry.'

From that day, Allardyce, a natural communicator and by this stage in his managerial career one of football's biggest celebrity managers, refused to take part in any BBC interviews before or after games. In December he was vindicated when Lord Stevens announced the interim findings of his Quest team's nine-month inquiry, which effectively gave the game a clean bill of health, though Stevens did say that 17 transfers – out of 362 – still required further investigation because eight football agents had failed to co-operate.

Despite the media scrum surrounding the club in the wake of the *Panorama* programme, on the field the players remained focused, organised and disciplined. Their first major test of the campaign came at the end of September when Liverpool, revitalised under Rafa Benitez, visited the Reebok. Benitez was to leave a beaten man as goals from Campo and man-of-the-match Speed gave Wanderers a deserved 2–0 win. Seven games into the season, Wanderers were second behind Chelsea. Wins at Newcastle and Blackburn Rovers – where Jussi Jaaskelainen saved two penalties in the dying moments – kept up the momentum, but there was a reality check in the shape of

Net profit: Spaniard Ivan Campo guides the ball home to set up a win against Liverpool.

Wayne Rooney and Manchester United looming. United blitzed Wanderers 4–0 at the Reebok with a stunning, attacking display. Still, despite the defeat, Wanderers had collected 20 points from their first 10 games.

With a record points haul for the club in the Premier League for that stage of the season, it didn't matter that Anelka was still to break his goalscoring duck in the Premier League, but after the United mauling Wanderers lost to Wigan and Everton and drew 2–2 at Sheffield United, despite having led 2–0.

'We had a run of matches where we had dominated the opposition and played some of our best football but failed to convert our chances,' says Allardyce. 'One of the most disappointing results was against Everton. We completely controlled the game from start to finish and we missed chance after chance after chance. In the end we lost 1–0 following an Arteta goal. If you don't take your chances you can pay the ultimate price.

'I also felt that the players had just lost the focus on getting clean sheets because they were playing so well in possession. They were expressing themselves so well that they'd forgotten that when they lost possession they needed to get back in there and make life difficult for the opposition.

Gunning for you: Nicolas Anelka scores his first Bolton League goal against his old club Arsenal.

Ball winner: midfield man Ivan Campo became an established crowd favourite at the Reebok.

'So, while it's always lovely to see your team dominate a game of football in possession, it's no good at the end of the game if you haven't got the win. This business is all about winning.'

When Wanderers welcomed Arsene Wenger's Arsenal side to the Reebok on 25 November, they had gone without a win for more than a month and their record signing was still searching for his first League goal in a Bolton shirt.

'There were questions being asked about Nicolas and the fact that he hadn't scored a goal for us,' says Allardyce. 'There was some

Nick of time: Anelka scores a magnificent second against Arsenal – set up by Campo.

rubbish being talked about in the media, asking if he was going to produce his best for us. We had actually started the season superbly, keeping five clean sheets in the first eight games, and that was the most important thing to begin with. The more clean sheets you get the more wins you get. So, although Nicolas wasn't scoring at that particular time, there was always somebody else popping up with a goal, and we were winning matches for fun. Then, all of a sudden, we stopped doing that and the pressure was heaped onto us.

'The Arsenal game was a real cracker.

Abdoulaye Faye gave us the perfect start with a goal after just nine minutes. It came from a corner into the box – we knew that if we could get good delivery in that area they would struggle, because it's always been a particular weakness of Arsenal's.

'Then close on half-time Nicolas scored. The great thing about the goal, his first Premier League goal for the club, was the quality of it; it was stunning. Kevin Davies hit a long ball out to him on the left and then we saw his trademark. He cut in from the left-hand side and from outside the box hit a screamer that gave Lehman no chance. The

Christmas present: Nolan celebrates after a Newcastle own-goal gifts Bolton a lifeline on Boxing Day.

disappointing thing was that we all got so carried away with celebrating, myself included, they kicked-off and scored to make it 2–1. But then in the second half Nicolas scored a second goal after a quality pass from Ivan Campo. His second wasn't quite as breathtaking, but it highlighted his pace.'

The 3–1 win enhanced Wanderers'

Emerging talent: Andranik – scoring against Wigan – made his mark in the second half of the season.

impressive record against Arsenal under Allardyce. 'Tactically, we had managed to outwit Arsene Wenger and his men for a few years. The fact that we were better tactically was overlooked, but how else do you explain the results when we had fewer resources, smaller facilities, fewer players and fewer quality players? Some people deem it a non-tactical approach, but actually it is down to astute planning. We set out a game plan to beat the opposition and we didn't always get credit for that.'

If that was a result to savour, then December was a month to feast on. Bolton notched five successive victories – which took them to third by the end of the year, above both Liverpool and Arsenal. Anelka, now firing, grabbed vital goals in four of those five games.

That run meant Wanderers could go into the second half of the season focused on European qualification – with 39 points already in the bag, Premier League survival was already assured.

Bolton went to Liverpool on New Year's Day knowing that if they could avoid defeat they could strengthen their grip on third spot. But Liverpool ended the Wanderers' winning streak with an emphatic 3–0 victory.

If December had been a feast, January was a famine as the side failed to register a League win. The FA Cup provided some relief when

Andranik Teymourian – an Iranian signed in the summer after an impressive World Cup – scored twice in a 4–0 win at Doncaster. The draw paired Bolton with Arsenal (again).

Bolton's impressive record against Wenger's men and their lofty League position seemed to underline the progress the club had made. Few were surprised when Bolton went to Arsenal and earned a replay with a battling display in a 1–1 draw.

The replay was a classic. Arsenal, quick out of the traps, were unstoppable in the first half. They led 1–0 at the break but in truth it should have been more. But Wanderers, resilient to the last, forced extra-time when Abdoulaye

Old pals: Anelka on the score sheet against Arsenal again, but this time it was in vain.

Precious point: Kevin Davies scores to give Bolton a draw at title-chasing Chelsea.

Meite scored with a header in injury-time. The tie appeared to be swinging Bolton's way. Kevin Nolan hit a post in extra-time, but then Arsenal grabbed the victory through Freddie Ljungberg and Emmanuel Adebayor.

'I thought it was going to be a classic Cup victory,' recalled Allardyce. 'Instead, it turned out to be a classic Cup tie that we lost.'

The Cup exit meant the main focus was on European Cup qualification. Wenger's men were having a disappointing League campaign by their own standards which left the door to the Champions League ajar for Wanderers. But a worrying loss of form put even UEFA Cup qualification in doubt.

To make matters worse, Wanderers were also hit by one of their worst injury crises for years. Nicky Hunt, Abdoulaye Faye, Tal Ben Haim, Kevin Nolan, El-Hadji Diouf and Stelios were all out injured for the trip to title chasing Chelsea on Saturday 28 April. But that was nothing compared with the bombshell that was about to hit the club.

For the matchday dawned with national newspaper headlines screaming 'Big Sam To Quit'. Despite the 'news', Allardyce took his seat as usual in the dug-out. Big Sam even barked out orders as usual from the touchline. Somehow his injury-ravaged side took the lead through debutant defender

All over bar the shouting: Big Sam on the touchline at Chelsea – his last game in charge of the side.

Double act: Sam Allardyce and Phil Gartside, who had been so close for more than seven years, were about to part company.

Lubomir Michalik. And even when Chelsea hit back to take the lead, the team showed their characteristic fighting spirit to level again through Kevin Davies. The game finished 2–2. In the circumstances, given the injuries and the build-up, it was a remarkable performance and a precious point. However, the club was significantly silent on the reports of Allardyce's future.

The following 48 hours were the most traumatic for Bolton Wanderers since October 1999. On Sunday 29 April, after a meeting between manager and chairman, Allardyce and the club released official statements announcing that one of the club's most successful managers in the modern era was resigning.

In his statement, Allardyce said 'The decision to leave the football club, which has been my spiritual home for over 18 years, as both player and manager, is one of the hardest I have had to make in my life. However, after guiding the team into a position where the club is on the verge of qualification for European football for the second time in three years, which has been the accumulation of almost seven years of strategic building and hard work across all areas of the football club, I feel it is the right moment to step down from my duties and welcome a new exciting era for the club under different leadership.

'I feel the club is in a great position to continue its upward trajectory with a talented, internationally recognised squad, supported by an excellent academy programme across all ages, working under the guidance of a highly-skilled football management team. I believe the foundation of the next phase for the next development stage of the club is well and truly in place. It is with this knowledge that I feel confident that I am moving on with my life, content with a legacy that I have tried to create for this special club, and I wish the owner, chairman, staff, players and above all the fans every success in the future.'

Chairman Phil Gartside said 'Since joining the club as manager in October 1999, he has helped lead a fantastic transformation of the club and has helped design and build an infrastructure that will enable the club to continue the progress that we have undoubtedly made in his period of office.'

The timing of the decision, with two games of the season to go, and European

New man in the hot seat: new manager Sammy Lee is greeted by chairman Phil Gartside less than 24 hours after Allardyce's resignation is announced.

qualification still in the balance, was curious to say the least. Questions remained as to exactly why Big Sam had chosen to go and what would happen to the side in the wake of his decision. The club acted swiftly to answer the latter. The football world was still rocking when Bolton called a press conference at 11am on 30 April to announce Allardyce's successor.

Less than 24 hours after Big Sam had gone, his assistant Sammy Lee was named as the new man in charge. The chairman revealed that the succession had always been part of the club's long-term thinking, though all concerned admitted the timing of the departure had caught them on the hop. As to why Allardyce had chosen that moment to leave when he still had two years left on his contract – and two games to go that season – remained a mystery, though it wasn't long before he was linked with other clubs, both Manchester City and Newcastle United figuring prominently.

Gartside was swift to reject a suggestion that Allardyce's departure from the Reebok was down to a lack of financial backing. 'There was some speculation that it was over a lack of funds, but we've finished in the top 10 of the Premier League for the last three years and

were on course to do so again, so there must have been some funds available,' he says.

'Football is all about success and we've been successful. Look at the position of the club. I would like somebody to tell me what we could have done better than where we are now. Look at how much Arsenal, Liverpool, Manchester United and Chelsea spend on players. The difference between finishing fifth in the League and finishing fourth in the League isn't £5m or £10m. It's £100m.

'We work within our resources, and I think it's a fantastic job that the staff have done at Bolton to achieve what has been achieved with limited resources. But those limited resources are based on what we can afford to put in and everything that is generated by the football club is put back into the football club.'

Lee's appointment may have been swift, but it was overshadowed by the dramatic exit of the man who had shaped the club's success for the best part of eight years. Few doubted Lee's ability on the training pitch, but his lack of a track record in management was immediately questioned. All this and the small matter of trying to clinch a UEFA Cup spot in the last two games were Lee's immediate inheritance.

'I know I have got a tough act to follow, but

one of the reasons I came to the club two years ago was that I was told then I would be considered, if the job ever came up. So it's no good being afraid now that I've been given the job,' he told the waiting press.

'I've never been daunted by anything in football. I've always wanted to face challenges, both as a player, as a coach and now as a manager. I have come into a situation where there's a great back-up team. There's an awful lot of work been done here so, if it's not broken, don't fix it. There are certain things I would like to try and influence. It would be wrong of me to come in and just try to be a clone of Sam. But Sam has built a solid base, alongside the chairman and alongside the owner, and I think it is important that we keep that.'

Despite the fact that Allardyce had become synonymous with Bolton Wanderers for the best part of a decade, Lee felt that the squad would get over the shock departure fairly quickly. Footballers tend to come and go. 'It's a transitory business,' he explained. One of his first decisions was to ask veteran midfield man Gary Speed to join the coaching staff as a player-coach.

With barely enough time to catch his breath, Lee was picking the team for his first game –

away at West Ham, who were fighting against relegation. In truth, because of the injury situation the team more or less picked itself.

But Lee's managerial career couldn't have got off to a worse start. His side were 3–0 down with just 29 minutes gone. Speed pulled a goal back in the second half but couldn't stave off a defeat. The only bright spot came with the news that, thanks to other results, Wanderers still had control of their own destiny.

Wanderers went into the final game of the season at home to Aston Villa knowing a win would be enough to earn a UEFA Cup spot for the second time in three seasons. However, they also went into it having won just four League games since the turn of the year.

In the meantime, reports that Allardyce was about to be appointed manager at an underachieving Newcastle United hardened as the Magpies announced they were ending Glenn Roeder's tenure as manager with just one game to go.

Yet again, Wanderers went into the final game of the season with their entire year's efforts on the line. Success would bring European football – failure would increase the pressure on Lee, just two games into his managerial career. Welcome to the world of

Kevin Nolan celebrates with his baby daughter as Bolton clinch a European spot in the final game of the season.

Happy Lee: new boss Sammy Lee sets his sights on Europe after getting the result he needed on the final day.

football management where you are only as good as your last result.

Lee knew the requirement. Wanderers had to match or better the results of Reading and Portsmouth to ensure at least seventh place in the table when they took on Martin O'Neil's Aston Villa side.

In a strange twist, Allardyce, fresh from talks over a multi-million pound contract with Newcastle, took up the chairman's offer to attend the game and took his usual seat in the Reebok stand alongside Gartside.

Lee opted for a 4–4–2 formation – rather than Allardyce's trusty 4–5–1 – and Speed gave Wanderers a first-half lead only for Villa to level

before the break. After the interval, Davies once more put Bolton in front, but once again they were pegged back. With Reading and Portsmouth also being held, a draw would be good enough. Wanderers held on for a 2–2 at the final whistle. But the season wasn't over. Not quite.

As the players left the field they gathered at the entrance of the tiny communications office where press officer Danny Reuben was waiting for confirmation of the result from Ewood Park. Reading and Blackburn Rovers were tied 3–3 as the game entered injury time.

The whole season was in the balance. There was nothing the players could do now but wait. The seconds were agonising. Then came the news from Ewood. A draw. Then jubilation.

The players went crazy. Cameras snapped. Wives were embraced. Children hugged. Champagne flowed.

It was a fitting way to bring the curtain down on the first 10 years of Reebok football. Just another average day of drama, tension, intrigue and joy at a stadium that has been built for it. The football wasn't bad either!

10 Year Record

1997-98:	18th in the Premier League, (relegated)
1998-99:	6th in Division One (Play-off Final runners-up)
1999-00:	6th in Division One (Play-offs)
2000-01:	3rd in Division One (promoted)
2001-02:	16th in the Premier League
2002-03:	17th in the Premier League
2003-04:	8th in the Premier League
2004-05:	6th in the Premier League
2005-06:	8th in the Premier League
2006-07:	7th in the Premier League

2006–07

Ins

Nicolas Anelka (Fenerbahce), Quinton Fortune (Manchester United), Abdoulaye Meite (Marseille), Idan Tal (Maccabi Haifa), Andranik (Abu Moslem), David Thompson (Portsmouth).

Outs

Jared Borgetti (Al-Ittihad), Khalilou Fadiga (Coventry City), Radhi Jaidi (Birmingham City), Hidetoshi Nakata (Retired), Bruno N'Gotty (Birmingham City).

Roll of Honour

Anthony Ainsworth
Julie Ainsworth
Anthony Ainsworth Senior
Roy, Judy, Gil, Andy Anton
Anthony Ashcroft
John Ashcroft
Dan, Oliver & Ian Barnes
Janet Barnett
Cath Bint
Kevin Blackburn
Derek Boardman
Ian Boardman
Tommy Boardman
Alan Bolton
Howard Booth
Mike & Merritt
Borrowman
David Boughton
Steven Boughton
David Brandwood
Florence Brandwood
Raymond Briggs
Christian Briggs
,Broadfoot Family

David Bromley
Tony Broxton
Alex Buchannan
Michael Burry
Philip Burry
Stanley Burton
Michael Cheetham
Susan Child
Zara Child
Paul Clarke
Toby Clinton
Douglas Clinton
Michael Coglan
Peter Coglan
Neil & Christopher Collier
Graham Compton
Joseph James Compton
Olive & Bill Cranshaw
Tony & Paul Cranshaw
Paul Crompton
Julie Crompton
Michael Crosbie
David Croughton
Christina Cunningham

Isabelle & Eleanor Dalton
Mark & Lisa Dalton
Mitchell Dalton
Patrick Dalton
Pat Davey
Eddie Davies
The Delaney Family
The Denham Family
Michael Dewhurst
J Dillon
Cheryl Doran
Malcolm Doran
John Alexander Doust
David Eastham
John Raymund Eastham
Graham Edge
Chris Edge
Steve Ellison-Houston
Sam Ellison-Houston
Ben Ellison-Houston
Kath England
Gareth Evans
David Fairclough
Lynn Farrimond

Brian Firth
Paul Foley
JJ & E Foley
Margaret Frith
Tom, Alex, Ste & Val Fryer
Carol Fryer
Ryan Furlong
Rebecca Kate Gardiner
Anne Gardiner
Neil Gardiner
Tony Garner
Paul Granville-Hankinson
Sue Green
Lee Greenwood
Jessica-Louise Haines
Gordon J Hall
Roland & Shirley Hallmark
Jack Hampson
Bet Hancarr
Mark Heys
Gabrielle Heys
Imogen Heys
Phil Heys (Sky Fanzone)
Norman William Heyworth
Gaynor Higson
David Hilton
Roger Hindle
Joe Carol Hodgkinson
Louise Natasha Hodgkinson
Liam Emma Hodgkinson
George Hodgson
David Holmes
Steven Honour
Thomas Honour
John Hughes
Maldwyn Hughes
Stephen Charles Hunt
Christine Isherwood
Benny Jensen
Daniel Jensen
Roy Johnson
Gillian Jones
Alan Kay
Gill Kay
Bradley Adam Kay

Andrew James King
Carlton Kirkpatrick
Andrew Knee
Geoff Knee
Andrew Knowles
Derek James Latham
Michael Latham
Stanley Lee
Harry Leek
Norman Lewis
Audrey Lewis
Jenny Lewis
Stefan Lewis
Jack Leyland
Gareth Lindsay
Wayne Llloyd
Alex Lowe
Matthew Madill
Bill Madill
Keith Makin
Roderick James Mark-Bell
George Mark-Bell
Mark Marsden
James Marsden
Dave Marsden
David W Marsh
Charles McFadden
Ann-Marie McFadden
Wayne McFadden
Roderick Middleton
Joseph Minihane
James Miskell
Carl Navarro
Helen Navarro
Holly Jayne Navarro
Caitlin Leah Nelson
John Nelson
Martin Nisbet and family
Emma Norris
Dave Norris
Janice Norris
Ray O'Donnell
Eric Graham Parkinson
Chris Parry
Christopher Peacock
Robert Peacock

Alan Pendlebury
Scott & Barry Pepper
John Pietralski & Family
Roy Platt
David Platt
Richard Poole
V & D Pope
Dennis Price
Paul Rainford
Gretta Rainford
Tom Rainford
William Hugh Ramsden
Jeremy Ian Ramsden
Shaun Ranshaw
Mark John Richardson
Eileen Rigby
Thomas Robert
Barbara Robinson
Martin Rushton
Paul Sayles
Ian Sayles
Stephen Shannon
Robert Sharpe
Stanley Shaw
Nigel & Gordon Sheppard
Allan Sheppard
Dave Sheppard
Ken Sheppard
Alan Simkin
Amanda Simmonds
John Simmonds
Alec Simmons
Neil Simmons
Nigel Simon
Lee Simpson
Beki Simpson
John P Simpson
Bernard Slater
Jane Smith
Kirsty Smith
Eric Spencer-Smith
Rab & Lochlyn Stewart
Ron Stockton
Philip Styan
Colin Styan
Brian & Charlie Sweeney

Geoff Swift
Mark Swift
Christine Taylor
Steve Taylor
Martin Timothy
Mark James Topham
Philip James Topham
Jim Unsworth
Derek Valentine
Neil Thomas Valentine
Matthew Neil Valentine
Bob Vickers
Joshua Walker
Charlotte Walsh
Louise Walsh
Councillor John Walsh OBE
Michael Walton
Malcolm Warburton

Lesley Ann Weatherall
Jack West Green
Andrew Peter Whitehead
Martin Ian Whitehead
Colin Graham Whitehead
Peter Graham Whitehead
David Graham Whitehead
Adrian Whittle
David Whittle
Ian Wilcock
Steven Wilkinson
Karen Wilkinson
Phil Wilkinson
Jon Williams
Ian Fletcher Wilson
Anthony David Wilson
David Ian Wilson
Katy Wilson

Malcolm Winrow
Gareth Winrow
David & Sue Wolfendale
Neil & Penny Wood
Veronica Wood
Josh Woodcock
Melvyn Woodcock
Neil Alexander Woodcock
Kathleen Anne Woodcock
Susan Worgan
Stuart Worthington
Robert Worthington
Michael & Jenny Yates
Sally & Lisa Yates
Takashi Yukoshi
Tomoko Yukoshi